Big World, Small Screen

Big World, Small Screen

The Role of Television in

American Society

Aletha C. Huston
Edward Donnerstein
Halford Fairchild
Norma D. Feshbach
Phyllis A. Katz
John P. Murray
Eli A. Rubinstein
Brian L. Wilcox
Diana Zuckerman

University of Nebraska Press
Lincoln and London

Copyright © 1992 by the
University of Nebraska Press
All rights reserved
Manufactured in the United
States of America
First paperback printing: 1993
Most recent printing
indicated by
the last digit below:
10 9 8 7 6 5 4 3 2 1
Library of Congress
Cataloging-
in-Publication Data
Big world,
small screen : the role of
television in
American society /
Aletha C. Huston . . .
[et al.]. p. cm. –
(Child, youth, and family
services)
Includes bibliograph-
ical references and index.
ISBN 0-8032-2357-9
ISBN 0-8032-7263-4 (pbk.)
1. Television and family –
United States.
2. Television and children –
United States.
3. Television audiences –
United States.
4. Television – Psychological aspects.
5. Television broadcasting –
Social aspects –
United States.
I. Huston, Aletha C.
II. Series. HQ520.B54 1992
306.85'0973-dc20
91-13520 CIP

∞

Contents

Preface

In 1986, the American Psychological Association (APA) appointed a task force to undertake a review of the literature on television and society. The members were: Aletha C. Huston, Chair, Edward Donnerstein, Halford Fairchild, Phyllis Katz, John P. Murray, Eli A. Rubinstein, and Diana Zuckerman. Norma Feshbach was a liaison from the APA Public Information Committee. Brian Wilcox was the APA staff liaison in the Public Affairs Directorate.

The charges to the task force were:

1. Review and integrate existing research on the positive and negative effects of television advertising and programming on particular segments of the United States population, specifically women, children, minorities, and the elderly. Emphasize research since the 1982 report from the National Institute of Mental Health, which updated the 1972 Report of the Surgeon General's Scientific Advisory Committee on Television and Social Behavior.

2. Make specific recommendations regarding additional areas of research needed to provide a more complete overview of the positive and negative effects of television on the targeted groups.

3. Make specific recommendations about how to remediate the most critical negative influences and how to enhance the most positive influences of television on the targeted groups.

4. Make specific recommendations on how the APA and the television industry, government, and scholarly groups may work together to improve the mental health aspects of television that affect the targeted groups.

5. Stimulate efforts to locate funding to support and disseminate the findings.

During the course of two years and four meetings, the task force members prepared an extensive review of the available literature on topics pertinent to the charges. Each member took primary responsibility for one or more sections; group discussions served to integrate findings and resolve contradictions. Questions about federal policy were addressed not only by reviewing the scholarly literature, but by interviewing representatives of the Federal Communications Commission and Action for Children's Television. Producers, writers, and media psychologists were also interviewed to obtain the industry's perspective on ways that psychologists and other professionals could work to improve television content. This book is an outgrowth of the task force report submitted to the American Psychological Association.

The sections of the book were originally prepared by different members of the task force; the final report of the task force to the APA was a joint document. For this book, the report was edited extensively, and transition and theoretical integrations were added by the first author with help from John Murray. Because there are many authors of the work, credit for individual sections is given here. Aletha Huston prepared the initial drafts for the sections on children, cognitive skills and prosocial behavior, nutrition and health, forms of television, effects of the medium, and public policy. Edward Donnerstein prepared the sections on sexuality and on new technologies. Halford Fairchild wrote the drafts of the sections on minority groups. Norma Feshbach, in collaboration with her associate, Peter Kovaric, wrote the sections on emotion and advertising. Phyllis Katz prepared the materials on gender and on gays and lesbians. John Murray wrote the initial drafts on violence, television and the family, the economics of television, and policy. Eli Rubinstein prepared the materials on the elderly and on institutionalized populations. Brian Wilcox served as an overall editor and coordinator of the literature review. Diana Zuckerman wrote the sections on social issues and on media literacy training. We also thank John C. Wright, University of Kansas, for contributing materials on television and the elderly.

Several people were essential to the preparation of the manuscript. Alison Dishinger, Vicki Hamlin, and the clerical staff at the APA all made major contributions to typing and editing. Vicki Hamlin prepared some of the graphs.

Introduction

★

In its approximately 40 years as a part of American society, television has become an integral part of almost every home. It accompanies much of daily life, either as foreground or as background. Opinions about the importance of television in modern society cover almost the entire range that one can imagine. Some social critics see its influences pervading every crevice of our lives, from our political decisions to our bedrooms. Some even argue that the medium of television produces basic changes in modes of thinking or induces a generally passive, intellectually lazy approach to dealing with the world. At the opposite extreme are those who consider television trivial and peripheral to the important ideas and human relationships in the world. They treat it as an innocuous medium of entertainment that is at worst irrelevant.

Despite the wide range of opinions about the importance of television, everyone agrees that it occupies a great deal of its viewers' time. Americans and people in most other countries spend many hours a week watching television. American children spend more time watching television than they do in school. Some of that "viewing" is accompanied by other activities—eating, playing, doing homework, and talking. Much of it occurs in the company of parents, siblings, and friends.

How do these hours with the television set influence children and adults? What impact has the medium had on daily life, family interaction, norms for behavior, and morality? Since the early days of television, social concern about its effects has generated research and periodic attempts to evaluate the literature in order to guide public policy. In 1972, the Surgeon General's Scientific Advisory Committee on Television and Social Behavior published a report titled *Television and Growing Up: The Impact of Televised Violence.* It was based on a five-volume set of research reports and reviews prepared expressly for the Committee's deliberations. Although this undertaking was unusually extensive for a government advisory board, its subject matter was limited. The title of the multivolume research report, *Television and Social Behavior,* in fact meant "television violence and aggressive behavior." The Surgeon General's Committee (1972) reached the conclusion that the evidence supported a "preliminary and tentative indication of a causal relation between viewing violence on television and aggressive behavior," with the qualifications that any such causal relation operates only on children predisposed to be aggressive and only in some environmental contexts (p.11).

Ten years later, the National Institute of Mental Health (1982) published an update of research titled *Television and Behavior,* which was accompanied by a second volume of technical reviews of the literature (Pearl, Bouthilet, & Lazar, 1982). Although the update did not have the advantage of new research commissioned for its use, the reviews of the literature illustrated the wide range of topics under investigation. The major headings included cognitive and affective aspects of television, violence and aggression, social beliefs and social behavior, social relationships, health, and American society. Once again, the editors concluded that television plays an important role in the lives of children and adults in our society. Perhaps because of the wide range of topics included, however, few specific conclusions or implications were widely circulated in the field.

In the early 1980s, the American Psychological Association undertook a review of the literature on television and violence. As a result, the APA adopted the position that television violence has a causal effect on aggressive behavior (American Psychological Association, 1985). Although many psychologists were glad to see the APA joining other professional organizations in the quest for reduced violence on television, they felt that many other issues needed attention as well. Therefore, they proposed the formation of the APA Task Force on Television and Society. It was charged to (1) review and integrate existing research on positive and negative effects of television advertising and programming on particular segments of the United States population, specifically women, children, minorities, and the elderly; (2) make specific recommendations regarding additional research needed to understand the relation of television to the targeted groups; and (3) make recommendations about how to remediate the most critical negative influences and how to enhance the most positive influences of television on the targeted groups. This book is the product of the work and deliberations of that task force.

GUIDING THEMES

Three major themes define the subject matter of this book. First, we are concerned with the role of television in the lives of vulnerable and relatively powerless subgroups in American society. The initial charge to the task force was to examine the effects of programming and advertising on women, children, minorities, and the elderly. Although there are many differences among these subgroups, they have in common a relatively peripheral and low-power status in society. They hold fewer positions of prestige and influence, have lower average incomes, and are less well represented in the bastions of political and economic decision making than white young and middle-aged men.

Other groups (e.g., institutionalized populations) are included in some sections because they, too, are powerless. Children and institutionalized individuals are especially vulnerable because they sometimes lack the intellectual and social skills needed to evaluate and resist televised messages. They may also be more apt than other groups to watch television under conditions where someone else makes program choices and decides when the set will be turned on and off.

Children, the elderly, institutionalized persons, and some ethnic minorities watch television a lot, at least partly because alternative activities are limited by physical restrictions or lack of financial resources. Despite their involvement with television, most of these groups are not the principal audiences sought by commercial television distributors because they are not the most lucrative and desirable markets for advertisers. Therefore, we are particularly concerned with the ways in which television meets or fails to meet the needs of these groups and, at the same time, the ways in which television cultivates attitudes and opinions about them.

The second theme of the book is best described as "beyond violence and aggression." Although there is a brief summary of the literature on violence, the major purpose of this volume is to explore other domains of human behavior. Both theory and intuition suggest that television plays an important role in the development of many facets of attitude, emotion, social behavior, and intellectual functioning. Many people in the United States and in other countries are exposed to certain ethnic minorities only through television. They have no regular contact in daily life. Television is filled with dramas about human interactions—about family life, love, sexuality, emotion, and problem solving. Surely viewers carry away some of these messages and images to be used in their own interactions with others. Television is also filled with information and persuasive messages—public-service warnings about drugs and alcohol, educational material, and the ever-present advertisements. Do viewers use information gained from television, and do they act as the persuaders would have them act?

Our third theme is that television *can* have both positive and negative influences, depending on the types of programs made available and the ways in which viewers use those programs. The medium itself is not inherently good or bad, as some have argued (e.g., Winn, 1987). Television can and should offer opportunities for learning and experiencing a wide range of events and human conditions, even when it is designed for entertainment. It has the potential for teaching children academic and social skills, with such thoughtfully planned programs as *Sesame Street* and *Mister Rogers' Neighborhood*. It can provide the elderly with information, activity, and a sense of companionship. Members of minority groups can and do use television as a source of information about their own cultures and about social mores in the majority culture.

For many groups, including people in institutions, messages about health and positive ways of dealing with others can contribute in a good way to knowledge and behavior. People can learn prosocial forms of behavior—cooperation, helpfulness, sympathy, negotiation in conflicts, and persistence when things get difficult—just as they can learn antisocial behavior.

Despite television's potential for positive contributions to society, the vast majority of social commentary about it emphasizes its negative and harmful effects, with good reason. Much American programming is designed primarily to attract the largest audience to the messages of the sponsors. Programs often contain social stereotypes, violence, and other content selected for its immediate appeal to a targeted "market" of buyers (not viewers) rather than for its utility to a wide range of groups in the society.

Our failure to use the power of television to pursue positive goals deserves at least as much attention as we give to its exploitation by purveyors of socially harmful messages. Given the current concern about a poorly educated citizenry and our nation's reduced capacity to compete in the world economy, the potentials of television and the hazards associated with failing to use them are well worth examining. Most other developed nations use television more prudently than the United States does, particularly with regard to the welfare of their children. In this volume, we attempt to identify some means by which television serves or could serve important needs, particularly those of the populations on which we are concentrating.

In summary, three themes guide this work. First, we are concerned with the uses by and influences of television on certain populations—children, the elderly, women, and minorities. Second, we attempt to go beyond the issues of violence and aggression to consider a wide range of topics. Third, we examine both the positive and negative influences of the medium as it is and as it might be.

BASIC ASSUMPTIONS

Scholars and social critics agree on few propositions about the medium of television. The many authors of the present volume represent a range of opinions, but there are some basic assumptions on which we all agree.

First, as a former commissioner of the Federal Communications Commission once said, all television is educational television. Although television is often used for entertainment, it is always more than mere entertainment. Even when it is not intentionally designed to teach, it carries messages about social interactions and about the nature and value of groups in the society that can influence attitudes, values, and actions among its viewers. It serves as a source of information about the world, whether viewers seek entertainment or enlightenment.

A second assumption is that television often influences viewers by what Greenberg (1988) calls the "drip" model, a process of subtle and gradual incorporation of frequent and repeated messages. Because many effects of television on beliefs and attitudes occur in accretions over time, the fantasy world of television can cultivate a subtly pervasive view of the real world, in which television images are blended inextricably with other sources of information. This assumption is supported by the finding in many studies that the more television individuals watch, the more they believe and accept its messages about society. Gradual, cumulative influences of the medium are difficult to measure with available social-science methods; therefore, we find ourselves in the position of having a plausible but not proven set of conclusions about the influence of television on many of the domains of interest in this volume.

The third principal assumption is that the effects of television on any individual depend on the characteristics and goals of the viewer as well as the content of what is watched. The outcomes are a result of an interaction between the viewer and the medium (e.g., Greenberg, 1974). The viewer's levels of understanding, knowledge, motivation, personality, attitudes, and purposes for viewing affect how the television content is used and understood by that viewer. One implication of this assumption is that changing the effects of television depends on interventions with viewers as well as changes in what is available to view. Interventions with parents, media-literacy training for children, and television-awareness programs for adults can be useful in altering viewing patterns and in providing better understanding of what is viewed. At the same time, this assumption does not imply, as some broadcasters seem to assert, that the television industry has no responsibility for changing its product. Viewers interact with what is available. The content of the material broadcast remains a critical part of the equation that determines what viewers glean from their experiences with the medium.

HOW TOPICS WERE SELECTED

Undertaking a review of such a broad topic as television and society could lead either to multiple volumes or to superficial generalities without focus. The themes described earlier provided some general guidelines, but we elected to limit coverage further to a sample of topics representing a range of issues. We presume that the basic principles illustrated by the sample also apply to many areas not specifically discussed.

The topics selected had several elements in common: (a) they had special relevance for the population subgroups on which we were concentrating; (b) they were frequently mentioned by social scientists and others as potentially important, but had received relatively little scholarly attention; (c) they appeared often in popular beliefs about television; (d) policy and social action might be guided by information about them; and (e) one of the task force members had special expertise about a topic.

Because the impact of television is a function of both the medium and the individual viewer's interests and attributes, we begin in Chapter 1 with an examination of how television is used by the groups of special interest in the book: children, the elderly, ethnic minorities, women, and institutionalized populations. What functions does it serve in their lives? What do they bring to their viewing experiences, and what do they take from them? Is television meeting their needs?

Television can have both positive and negative effects on social stereotyping, self-perceptions and aspirations, and intergroup attitudes. In Chapter 2, the portrayals and messages conveyed by television about the population subgroups with which we are especially concerned are examined. For four groups—children, the elderly, minorities, and women—television messages are identified, and the literature on the effects of the television medium and its messages is summarized. A fifth group, gays and lesbians, is included as well because they represent another potential target of social stereotyping.

Television is a source of social and emotional learning—perceptions of social roles and acceptable social behavior and of positive and negative forms of social behavior (e.g., altruism, conflict-resolution strategies). In Chapter 3, literature is reviewed as it relates to four domains of social learning: family relations, emotion, sexuality, and violence.

Educational and persuasive uses of television are considered in Chapter 4. Planned programming can be effective in teaching cognitive skills and prosocial behavior. Public-service campaigns are sometimes useful ways of influencing behavior. Health messages can be transmitted on television. Advertising is the prime means by which television producers attempt to persuade; the effects of advertising on children is of special interest. At the same time, programs about such sensitive social issues as suicide may have the dual effects of raising consciousness about a problem and precipitating the very problem they are designed to identify.

In Chapter 5, the nature of the television medium itself—its forms and formats as distinct from its content messages—are considered. Social critics sometimes argue that television contributes to a variety of ills, including intellectual passivity and laziness, poor school achievement, and lack of creativity. A large body of literature on children's attention to and comprehension of television indicates that children are intellectually active during viewing. Forms and formats of television can be used judiciously to increase or decrease children's mental effort and learning from television.

People do not watch television in a vacuum. They often watch television in social contexts, and what they watch is limited by the available programming. In Chapter 6, we examine two dimensions of the television-viewing environment. One of these is the social and educational environment in which children learn to watch television. Parental and family influences on viewing are considered, and planned interventions to train children in media literacy are discussed. The other dimension is the programming available. Technological changes, including cable and videorecorders, vastly expanded the selection of programs available to many people during the 1980s. The impact of these technological changes on viewing and on what is available to view are discussed.

One of the goals of this volume is to offer suggestions for public policy regarding television. Toward this end, in Chapter 7, we examine the economic basis of television in the United States as it compares with other industrialized countries. We discuss some of the issues on the federal policy agenda during the last several years, and offer some proposals for both public policy and private advocacy to improve television content in ways that serve the needs of impoverished and powerless groups in American society.

In the final chapter, we summarize the conclusions from earlier chapters and make proposals for needed research, identifying some of the important issues that could benefit from careful investigation in the coming decade.

How People Use Television

❶

The role that television plays in people's lives depends not only on the content transmitted, but on the goals and interests of the individual viewer (Palmgreen, Wenner, & Rosengren, 1985; Rosengren, Wenner, & Palmgreen, 1985). It is one-sided to describe the effects of television as though they made an impact on essentially passive viewers. People use television to serve many functions. For people of all ages, being entertained and receiving information are the two reasons given most often for viewing, but relaxation, sociability, time filling, and many other functions are served by the medium (Blumler & Katz, 1974; Condry, 1989).

Although television is used for many purposes, one way of understanding differences in the total amount of viewing by various groups is the default hypothesis—that watching television is a default activity during times when an individual is at home (or near a television set) and not engaged in activities that conflict with viewing. Therefore, the amount of television viewed is a function of the time spent at home and the time required by alternative, incompatible activities. When people have limited financial resources, their opportunities for such alternative activities are also limited. When people are restricted from leaving their residence by health, immaturity, home responsibilities, or institutionalization, they have more time available to devote to television if they choose (Kubey & Csikszentmihalyi, 1990).

The default hypothesis provides a partial explanation for television use by different age groups, minorities, women and men, and people in institutions. Children, the elderly, and people in institutions have restricted mobility. Many members of minority groups are poor and cannot afford a wide range of alternative activities. Women spend more time at home than men because they are employed for fewer hours on the average. Not all television use can be explained as a default, but the broad parameters of viewing are established by these fundamental differences in opportunity to use television and opportunity for other activities.

In this chapter, we examine data on viewing patterns for children, the elderly, minorities, women, and institutionalized people, with attention to the amounts and types of programs chosen by each group. All of these groups are heavy users of television, but they are typically not the primary targets of television producers and programmers because they are not the most lucrative markets for advertisers. In many instances, therefore, available programming is not optimally designed to suit the needs of these diverse groups.

CHILDREN

Estimates of the average amount of viewing by children vary widely, depending on the method of assessment. Even by conservative estimates, however, the average American child watches television between two and three hours a day (Condry, 1989). This figure varies a great deal from child to child, but the amount of time that an individual child spends viewing is highly stable over time (Huston, Wright, Rice, Kerkman, & St. Peters, 1990).

Children begin "watching" television in infancy (Hollenbeck & Slaby, 1979; Lemish & Rice, 1987). Parents often report putting their babies in front of a television set to quiet them. Viewing increases rapidly during the preschool years, drops slightly at school entrance, then increases to a peak in early adolescence (around age 12). It declines in adolescence (see Figure 1.1) (Comstock, Chaffee, Katzman, McCombs, & Roberts, 1978; Huston et al., 1990; Liebert & Sprafkin, 1988). In Sweden, the mean levels of viewing are lower than in the United States, but the same age changes occur (Rosengren & Windahl, 1989).

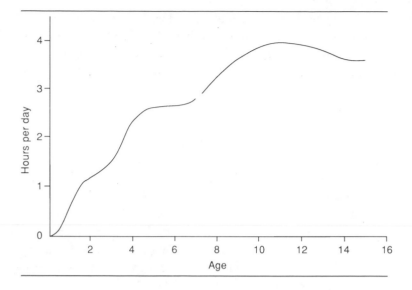

Figure 1.1. Estimated average hours of television viewing per day by age in the United States in 1987. From *The Early Window: Effects of Television on Children and Youth* (3rd Ed.) by R. M. Liebert and J. Sprafkin, 1988, New York: Pergamon, Figures 1.2, p.5. Reprinted by permission of Pergamon Press.

Although children spend a lot of time in the same room with an operating television set, there are only a few investigations that provide information about how much of that time they spend attending actively to the programming. Videotapes of home viewing, for example, show that children often play, eat, do homework, and talk when "watching" television (Bechtel, Achelpohl, & Akers, 1972). In one such investigation, attention to the set was indexed by the percentage of time the child looked at the screen. Children's attention to the set increased during the preschool years; by age 5 or 6, they looked at the set about 60% of the time it was on. The age trends are shown in Figure 1.2 (Anderson, Lorch, Field, Collins, & Nathan, 1986).

Changes in viewing habits as children grow older appear to result from changes in opportunity to view and from cognitive and social developmental changes. The drop in viewing around age 6 is probably a result of children's entering school and having

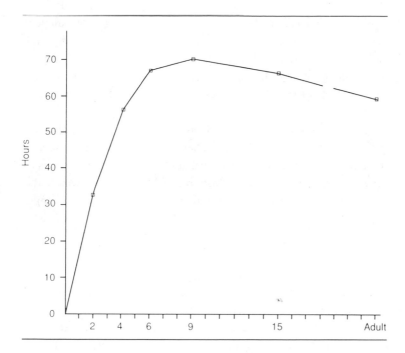

Figure 1.2. Percentage of visual attention to television as a function of age. The data are based on home observations of 208 children and 127 adults over ten days. From "Children's Attention to Television: Implications for Production" by D. R. Anderson and D. E. Field, 1983, in M. Meyer (Ed.), *Children and the Formal Features of Television* (pp. 56–96), München: K. G. Saur, Figure 2. Reprinted with permission of K. G. Saur Verlag (München).

less time at home. From ages 3 to 7, children view programs that are increasingly complex and cognitively demanding, probably as a result of their improving comprehension abilities (Huston et al., 1990). Throughout middle childhood, children are allowed to stay up later and they become increasingly able to understand the plots and characters in standard entertainment comedies and dramas (Collins, 1983). During adolescence, children become more independent, spend more time away from home, and devote more time and interest to peer-related activities. One result is that popular music occupies some of the time spent earlier with television (Rosengren & Windahl, 1989).

Still another change with age is children's increasing independence from parents' controls and viewing choices. Most of young children's viewing of adult programs occurs in the company of their parents. As children get older, the amount of viewing with parents declines (St. Peters, Fitch, Huston, Wright, & Eakins, in press). Children seek entertainment from television, but they also use it for learning. At the preschool level, the average child spends three to five hours a week watching such informative programs as *Sesame Street* and *Reading Rainbow*. Older children watch relatively little informative programming, perhaps because fewer age-appropriate programs are available.

THE ELDERLY

The elderly watch more television than any other age group. They are sometimes described as "embracers of television" (Glick & Levy, 1962). Viewing increases up to about age 70, then declines some (Davis & Kubey, 1982; Harris and Associates, 1987).

The reasons for the increases in viewing with age are manifold. Some are obvious. The elderly are classed by Comstock et al. (1978) as "disadvantaged" people, who share with other disadvantaged groups a high rate of dependency on television for news, information, entertainment, and companionship. Davis (1975) lists the attractions and functions of television for the elderly as involvement, companionship, filling time, and structuring time. The latter refers to the role of television as a replacement for job, child-care, and homemaking routines in providing regular times each day for specific activities. The organization of the senior's day around a television schedule has been suggested as well by Myersohn (1961) and Schalinske (1968).

Television is a "parasocial activity" (Davis & Kubey, 1982) that "allows isolated older persons to maintain the illusion of living in a populated world" (p.202). Television can also fill specific gaps left by the death of a spouse or the distancing of a grown family (Frank & Greenberg, 1979).

The kinds of programming older people watch on television differ from those watched by younger and midlife populations. The most popular programs among the elderly, according to several surveys, are news, documentaries, and public-affairs programs (Davis, 1971; Wenner, 1976). Kubey (1980) suggests that such programming provides a social information network that is functionally equivalent to the informal network previously supplied by the workplace.

In any case the surveys agree that respondents tend to avoid much of the dramatic fare on television, with the exception of soap operas and situation comedies with sympathetic elderly characters. Adams and Groen (1974) and Bower (1973) both found that senior viewers prefer not only news and documentaries, but also variety shows, musical specials, travelogues, and quiz shows. Barton (1977) argues that daytime soaps supplant lost gossip networks, and the ratings confirm heavy viewing of them among the elderly. Senior stars, such as Bob Hope, Lawrence Welk, and George Burns are also extremely popular with seniors (Davis & Kubey, 1982).

ETHNIC MINORITIES

In general, low-income people watch more television than those with high income, and highly educated people watch less television than people with less formal education. Therefore, many ethnic minorities, who are disproportionately concentrated in low-income and lower educational brackets, are heavy television users (Comstock et al., 1978; Greenberg, 1986).

Television is particularly important in the lives of black Americans. They watch more television than whites, even when social class is controlled. Well-educated and young adult blacks are especially heavy viewers (Roberts & Bachen, 1981). Blacks have more favorable attitudes to television than whites, and they rely more on television for news and information (Comstock & Cobbey, 1982; Staples & Jones, 1985). Blacks tend to prefer programs featuring blacks; they are apt to perceive programs as reflecting reality; and they often use television to learn social codes of conduct (Brown, 1982; Greenberg, 1986).

Relatively little information exists about how television is used by other ethnic minorities, such as Hispanics, Asians, and Native Americans. At least partly because many members of these ethnic groups are poor, the average time spent using television is high. During the 1970s and 1980s, cable channels in various languages became available in most metropolitan areas. Univision, a Spanish-language channel, for example, is watched extensively by Hispanics. We know little, however, about how such television functions for adults or children. It may be a means of preserving their original language and culture, and it may at the same time isolate them from the wider society.

WOMEN

Two apparently contradictory patterns describe gender differences in viewing. Throughout childhood, boys watch more television than girls (Huston et al., 1990; Rosengren & Windahl, 1989; Singer & Singer, 1981). This difference does not appear to be a result of differing opportunities to watch television, but to the fact that some types of television content are more interesting to boys than to girls. Specifically, boys watch more cartoons, action adventure shows, news, and sports than girls (Huston et al., 1990; Rosengren & Windahl, 1989). The medium itself may also have greater appeal to males. When a television set is turned on, there is some tendency for boys and men to look at the set more than girls and women do, though there are not gender differences in recall of content (Alvarez, Huston, Wright, & Kerkman, 1988; Anderson et al., 1986). Boys seem to be especially attentive to programs with animation and high action (Alvarez et al., 1988).

By contrast, in adulthood, women spend more time watching television than men (Comstock et al., 1978). This difference appears to be at least partly explained by the default hypothesis. Women spend more time at home than men, so they have more opportunity to view. In one survey, women who were employed full-time watched less television than those who were not employed; their viewing times were similar to those of employed men. Not surprisingly, the differences occurred in program categories broadcast during the daytime—unemployed women watched more dramas, game shows, news, and talk shows than employed women. There were no differences between these groups of women in time spent viewing comedies and other types of programs that are broadcast primarily during the evening (Fitch, Huston, & Wright, 1990).

PEOPLE IN INSTITUTIONS

Institutionalized individuals also warrant special attention as television users, in part because they are often populations for whom professionals and government officials have direct responsibility. Because they are not a part of the vast audience of home viewers, these individuals have not been of much concern to either the television industry or the researchers studying the effects of television on the viewer. What little evidence is available suggests that they watch television extensively.

The persons involved represent populations at special risk. Whether they are mentally disturbed children or old individuals confined to an institution, they are especially vulnerable to the effects of television. They watch television even more than the general population. Moreover, the confining nature of the setting itself, whether a prison or a hospital, makes the nature of television viewing a more critical and less voluntary part of the daily activity than it is in the home.

The total number and diversity of persons in institutions at any one time is far from insignificant. They reside in homes for the aged, prisons and jails, hospitals, centers for the mentally ill, juvenile detention centers, residential treatment centers, shelters for the homeless, and various rehabilitation centers. While no exact count can be made, it is certain that the total number of individuals in these institutions is in the millions.

Despite their numbers, institutionalized people have not been the targets of extensive research. For example, one review examined the research on television use by the emotionally disturbed, the learning disabled, and the mentally retarded child. There were only a few studies dealing with these groups in residential settings (Sprafkin, Gadow, & Grayson, 1984).

What is most critical in considering television viewing by institutionalized children is not so much the need for lessening the negative effects, but the possibility of enhancing the positive potential of television. For example, nonhandicapped children can be influenced toward prosocial behavior by appropriate television viewing (Rushton, 1982). In the few studies of institutionalized children, the results typically showed that these young viewers also learned positive social skills (Sprafkin et al., 1984). Indeed, in some instances the learning was more pronounced than was the case in studies of normal children. In one such study (Rubinstein & Sprafkin, 1982), children in a residential facility for emotionally disturbed children were rotated through four treatments (a prosocial television diet with or without discussion, or a control television diet with or without discussion). The control diet consisted of programs without prosocial content. Children exhibited more altruistic behaviors after viewing the prosocial programming than after the control television diet.

There is an equally sparse body of literature on the effects of televised violence on the aggressive behaviors of institutionalized children. In reviewing that research, Sprafkin et al. (1984) note that the results confirm the findings in the much more extensive literature about normal children. All the studies of institutionalized youngsters, whether the children were delinquent, emotionally disturbed, or mentally retarded, found increased aggressive behavior following exposure to televised violence.

Television is also used a great deal by children hospitalized for physical illness. The only extended investigation of hospital viewing seems to be a project in Canada (Guttentag, Albritton, & Kettner, 1983). These investigators developed a closed-circuit television capability that provided programs especially selected for their positive informational content. People on the wards talked with children to answer questions. The children showed increased interest in the programming, and the hospital staff were very enthusiastic. This form of alternate programming has enormous potential for reducing boredom and making positive therapeutic and educational contributions to the treatment of hospitalized children.

We have limited knowledge about the viewing patterns or the effects of television viewing by institutionalized populations. What little we do know indicates that commercial television in its present form does almost nothing to address their special needs. Indeed, because these populations are at special risk and because they watch even more television than the normal, at-home population, television viewing has the potential for being a much more harmful activity for them than for the normal viewer. It also has the potential for positive contributions to these individuals' lives.

SUMMARY AND IMPLICATIONS

Many of the populations considered in this section are heavy users of television. Like most Americans, they use television for entertainment, but they also seek information, news, companionship, relaxation, and relief from boredom from the television set. Heavy use is partially explained by the default hypothesis—television viewing is a default option that is more apt to be pursued by people who spend many hours at home and who have relatively few alternative, incompatible activities available to them. For children, the elderly, minorities, institutionalized individuals, and some women, time at home is plentiful, and alternative activities are curtailed by financial and physical limitations. Hence, they turn to television more than some other subgroups.

Each subgroup also uses television in relation to its particular interests and abilities. As children grow older, they shift from simple to more cognitively demanding programs. Elderly people watch more news and informational programs and less dramatic fiction than other groups. Minorities often prefer programs portraying their own group and their own language background. Girls and women find cartoons, adventures, and sports less appealing than boys and men do; they also are somewhat less attracted to certain media techniques such as animation and high action.

Television has the potential to make positive contributions to each of these populations. Children can learn both academic and social skills. Television can also provide a window on the world beyond their immediate experience. Elderly people can gain knowledge about health, economic, and social issues as well as a sense of companionship. Members of minority groups can and do use television as a source of information about social mores in the majority culture and as a source of models from their own group. Institutionalized people can gain a sense of contact with the noninstitutional world and can learn a variety of skills from television.

Unfortunately, so far as commercial television is concerned, none of the populations discussed have the demographic attributes that would make them an attractive market. Disposable income in these segments of the population is far below average, as are all the other characteristics that are used to define the desirable commercial program audience. Precisely because they are not a market-driven audience, organized efforts need to be made to respond to their special needs. As the population of this country changes, it becomes increasingly important to attend to the needs of diverse groups. For example, with more than 20% of the American population now over age 55, the elderly are an influential part of our citizenry. Furthermore, they are the most rapidly growing segment of our population. Similarly, blacks, Hispanics, and Asians are an increasing percentage of the United States population, especially among families with children.

As a society, we have a special obligation to ensure that television serves our children and meets some needs of people in institutions because they are particularly vulnerable populations. They often lack the skills to evaluate and resist televised messages. They may be exposed to television under conditions where others decide when viewing will occur and what will be viewed. Parents, the administrators of mental institutions, and those caring for mentally retarded children, to mention only a few, have the responsibility to maximize the potentially positive role of television in the lives of these individuals.

Television Images and Their Effects

People are the stuff of television. The bulk of popular entertainment programs portray characters in comedic and dramatic situations selected to draw the largest and most affluent audiences. Whether it is intentional or not, the people shown are not representative of the populations who watch the programs. Gerbner (1972) describes entertainment television as a set of cultural indicators—symbolic representations of the power relations and human values of our culture. The groups shown most often are those with importance in the society. Power is further symbolized by roles in which characters exercise control over other characters and succeed in achieving their ends. According to this view, violence is one means of representing power; its symbolic meanings go well beyond the nature of violence per se.

In a related analysis, Clark (1972) proposed that the legitimacy of social groups is communicated in the mass media by two types of activities: recognition and respect. Recognition occurs when an individual identifies the existence of another by paying attention or taking that person into account. In the mass media, recognition of social groups occurs when they appear in programs. Conversely, groups of people who are underrepresented suffer from nonrecognition.

Respect is conferred when people identify with others by sharing their definitions of behavior, their assessments of behavior, and their explanations of behavior. Mass media encourage respect for social groups by showing them in roles that are sympathetic and positive—roles that make possible these forms of identifica-

tion. Conversely, respect is denied when social groups are portrayed in stereotyped or negatively valued roles.

If representation on television symbolizes power and social
recognition, then portrayals of the groups of concern in this volume need to be examined carefully. Children, the elderly, minorities, and women are often devalued in American society, and they
have relatively little power or disposable income by comparison
with white men. All except children have been the victims of
discrimination in employment and other domains of social and
economic activity. But, children have a higher probability of living
in poverty than any other age group in the United States because
they are the indirect victims of economic discrimination against
women and minorities. Gays and lesbians constitute still another
category of people that is often stigmatized.

Critics of television programming have made parallel observations about portrayals of several of these groups. In comparison
with their proportions in the population, children, elderly people,
minorities, women, and gays and lesbians are all underrepresented
in television programming. Stereotyped portrayals are frequent,
though the form of the stereotypes differs from group to group.
A small number of programs have successfully counteracted sex
and ethnic-group stereotypes.

Underrepresentation and negative portrayals may influence the
self-concepts and images of their own group for members of the
affected categories and may also generate attitudes and beliefs
about such groups among members of the general public. Gerbner
and his associates proposed that the constant themes of entertainment television subtly cultivate beliefs among its viewers
(Gerbner, Gross, Morgan, & Signorielli, 1986). Even when people
recognize that the material they are viewing is fictional, its messages and images gradually shape expectations and beliefs about
the real world.

Greenberg (1988) recently argued that this drip model of gradual accretion is incomplete. At times, one or two particularly
salient portrayals can have a dramatic effect on viewers' images
and beliefs—the "drench" hypothesis. One *Cosby Show* may have

more effect on viewers' images of blacks than many less memorable programs.

In this chapter, we examine how television presents children, the elderly, minority groups (specifically blacks, Hispanics, Asians, and Native Americans), women, and gays and lesbians. We then ask how such portrayals influence self-images and social attitudes about each group.

CHILDREN

There is a striking absence of writing about images of children on television or about the effects of these images on viewers. Early content analyses showed that children and adolescents constituted fewer than 10% of the characters in television dramatic fiction (Gerbner, 1972). In the last ten years, many prime-time situation comedies with children and adolescents as central characters have become extremely popular (e.g., *Growing Pains, The Cosby Show, Family Ties*), but recent content analyses show continued underrepresentation and devaluation of both children and adolescents (Signorielli, 1987).

Social commentators speculate about children's responses to these television images. For instance, children in the 1980s were shown as more mature and competent than their bumbling parents—a role reversal that could have some interesting outcomes. One hears anecdotes about early adolescents who watch *Growing Pains* because they think Mike Seaver is great, but virtually no data exist on children's reactions to these portrayals.

THE ELDERLY

Elderly people are underrepresented on television fiction and in most other categories of programming as well. When they are portrayed, negative stereotypes are often shown. Aging in females is portrayed more negatively than in males, and elderly females are particularly scarce on television (Davis & Davis, 1986; Davis & Kubey, 1982). The content analyses leading to these conclusions were conducted before the introduction of the popular comedy *Golden Girls.* If Greenberg's drench hypothesis is correct, these salient older women may have done more to change viewers' ideas about older women than the proportions of their on-air exposure would suggest.

A few studies indicate that negative attitudes toward elderly people are associated with television viewing (Davis & Kubey, 1982), but the evidence is scattered. Clear evidence for the effectiveness of television comes from an extensive evaluation of a planned program, *Over Easy,* designed to reach viewers 55 and older. The program fostered positive attitudes about aging, conveyed specific self-help information, encouraged related information seeking, and facilitated the use of social services in the viewers' communities (Keegan, 1983).

MINORITIES

Generalizations about ethnic minorities are limited by the fact that each minority group has unique characteristics. We have confined our discussion to four groups: blacks, Hispanics, Asians, and Native Americans. Since the invention of television, most ethnic minorities have been relatively absent from programming. When they were present, portrayals were often stereotypic or demeaning. Although most content analyses have focused on the portrayal of black Americans, portrayals of American Indians, Asians, and Hispanics are also frequently simplified caricatures (Berry, 1988; Berry & Mitchell-Kernan, 1982; Poindexter & Stroman, 1980).

After the civil rights and black power movements of the 1960s, the numbers of blacks in major and minor roles on television increased (U.S. Commission on Civil Rights, 1977). By the early 1980s, however, their numbers had declined to about 8%, less than their percentage of the American population. Hispanics constituted 3.5% of television characters, Asians were 2.5%, and Native Americans less than 1%. Within each ethnic group, women were particularly underrepresented; men outnumbered women by 3 to 1 in each group (Berry, 1980; Greenberg, 1986). Analyses that include nonfiction programming indicate little change in the proportions and status of minorities on television (Williams & Condry, 1989).

Ethnic minorities are concentrated in particular types of programs, primarily comedies. They are infrequently shown in children's programs and daytime serials (Barcus, 1983; Weigel & Howes, 1982). When they are portrayed, blacks are likely to be young. Most of the obese characters on television are black (Kaufman, 1980).

Cross-racial or cross-ethnic interactions are relatively infrequent because many shows are all white or all black. Portrayals of informal cross-race interactions occur with children and adolescents, but among adults, they tend to be more formal and distant than within-race interactions (Greenberg, 1986; Pierce, 1980; Williams & Condry, 1989).

Minority group members are also underrepresented in news programming, both as broadcasters and as subjects of the news. News stories about blacks and Hispanics are more often negative, focusing on crime or other negative attributes than are stories about whites (Greenberg, 1986).

Despite these overall patterns, two events worth mentioning occurred in the late 1980s. First, *The Cosby Show* became the most popular program on television. This program, which featured the lifestyles of an upper middle-class black family in a situation-comedy format, captured the nation's attention despite the fact that it challenged stereotypes about blacks. Second, blacks began winning significant positions in both dramatic television programming (e.g., *Miami Vice*) and in talk-show formats (e.g., the *Oprah Winfrey Show*). The effects of these recent trends have not been systematically investigated, but they point to some positive growth and development within the television industry (Bayles, 1985).

Effects of Television Portrayals of Minorities
Nonrecognition and negative portrayals of minorities have two potential outcomes: (1) the creation or maintenance of negative intergroup attitudes (i.e., prejudice and racism), and (2) negative effects on the self-esteem of members of the minority groups. Considerable evidence shows that blacks prefer and identify with

black characters, but there is relatively little information about the effects of such programs on their self-images (Graves, 1980; Meyer, Donohue, & Henke, 1978). White viewers enjoy programs portraying blacks about as well as those portraying whites, but we do not know how their attitudes about blacks or other minorities are affected by viewing blacks on television (Barry & Sheikh, 1977; Berry & Mitchell-Kernan, 1982; Greenberg, 1986). One investigation of adults' reactions to *All in the Family* demonstrated a large variation in responses. Adults who were initially prejudiced against blacks interpreted the program as supporting their views and those with low levels of prejudice thought that the program reinforced nonprejudicial attitudes (Vidmar & Rokeach, 1974).

A small but growing body of literature has documented the potential role of television in reversing negative self-perception and intergroup attitudes and behaviors (cf. Fairchild, 1988; Laosa, 1976). For example, the positive interactions of different ethnic groups on *Sesame Street* led to an increase in positive intergroup attitudes among preschool children (Gorn, Goldberg, & Kanungo, 1976). Other investigations have shown that prosocial interactions and nonstereotypic portrayals can lead to cooperation, reduction in prejudice, reduction in traditional sex-role attitudes, and good citizenship (Calvert & Huston, 1987; Johnston & Ettema, 1982).

WOMEN AND GENDER ROLES

Content analyses conducted through 1980 agree on a number of conclusions. First and foremost, portrayals of males outnumber those of females (with the possible exception of daytime soaps). Males are shown as major characters on the average of three times as often as females on prime-time television. Proportions vary with the type of program. The male-to-female ratio was about 6 to 1 in action-adventure shows, 2 to 1 in situation comedies, and 9 to 1 in commercial voice-overs (Greenberg, 1988). The effects of this underrepresentation of females have not been assessed, but concern has been expressed about possible messages of devaluation of females, absence of role models, and potential for stereotyping

(Butler & Paisley, 1980; Calvert & Huston, 1987; Feshbach, Dillman, & Jordan, 1979; Williams, Baron, Phillips, Travis, & Jackson, 1986).

Before 1980, other repeatedly documented findings showed that women were depicted as being considerably younger than men, were less frequently shown in work situations, had more restricted vocational roles, and were often portrayed as being passive, dependent on men, and overly concerned with their physical appearance. As Feshbach, Dillman, and Jordan (1979) concluded, "The model female on television is a young adult, beautiful, dependent, helpless, passive, concerned with interpersonal relations, warm, and valued for her appearance rather than for her capabilities and competencies, personal and professional" (p.376).

Some changes may have occurred since 1980, at least with regard to prime-time and daytime programs, but no consensus exists. A series of studies undertaken by the National Commission on Working Women (1982, 1984, 1985, 1986a, 1986b) of new prime-time shows since 1981 suggest that women's roles on prime-time television have at least become more varied, interesting, and vocationally involved. In the spring of 1986, for example, the proportion of women depicted as working outside of their home was about two thirds, which matched the census statistics for the same period. Prime-time-frequency statistics apparently improved in American television in 1984, when females constituted 47% of the characters on new programs. This trend, noted by the NCWW did not continue unabated, however, and was not corroborated in other contexts (e.g., Durkin, 1985a; Williams et al., 1986). The NCWW survey of 1985 and 1986 prime-time shows revealed a decrease in the number of female characters, an increase in the number of shows that were exclusively male, and a return of women to the role of victim in action and detective stories. Moreover, recent studies suggest that the frequency of showing women on both American and Canadian television may not be very different from earlier ratios (Davis, in press; Williams et al., 1986).

American prime-time television now shows more women who are interesting and autonomous than it used to (Meehan, 1988).

Occupational roles presented are, however, less traditional for women than for men (cf. Williams et al., 1986). In fact, some commentators have noted that these fantasy females may be far removed from the reality of most women's lives. For example, almost one quarter of the women shown on television in 1984 were extremely affluent, whereas in reality only 0.2% of women earned over $75,000 a year. A much higher proportion of working women are shown in professional and entrepreneurial roles than actually exist. Moreover, despite the increased portrayal of working women, these women rarely experience problems with child care, sex discrimination, harassment, or poverty. Older women have become more interesting recently to television producers. Here, too, the picture is mixed. Although women over 40 are now seen more frequently, they do not look or act older than those under 40.

In short, portrayals of prime-time women have definitely improved, perhaps so much so that they are far removed from the world of reality. If women characters are not representative, however, it may be best to err on the positive side because such role models may contribute to high levels of aspiration. The danger, of course, is that new stereotypes about well-off women on television may cause the viewing public to ignore the very real problems that women continue to face in this society.

The changes in images of women on prime-time network programming are not necessarily reflected in other program types (Calvert & Huston, 1987; Davis, in press; Williams et al., 1986). A recent study by Davis analyzing all network shows presented in the spring of 1985 notes that women are still younger, blonder, and less frequently seen than men. Gender roles on many children's programs, especially cartoons, continue to be extremely stereotyped. Missing from most content analyses are news, talk shows, and public service programs watched by children. Although it would appear that female commentators are now de rigueur, the few detailed analyses conducted of such programs (cf. Williams et al., 1986) suggest that anchors, reporters, interviewers, and experts presented are still overwhelmingly male.

Effects of Gender Portrayals

In contrast to the extensive descriptions of sex roles on television, there are very few studies in which the direct effects of television portrayals on children or adults are assessed. Correlations between television viewing and stereotyped beliefs appear fairly consistently. Zuckerman, Singer, and Singer (1980), for example, demonstrated that children's viewing practices were related to the degree of racial and gender prejudice they exhibited. Girls who watched the most television had the most negative attitudes toward their gender. In other studies significant relationships between frequency of television viewing and degree of sex-role stereotyping have also been found (e.g., Durkin, 1985b; Frueh & McGee, 1975; McGee & Frueh, 1980). In one recent study (Katz & Coulter, 1986) children's stereotyping was related to type of media preferences. Those who watched a lot of television were strongly gender-stereotyped, whereas children who read a lot were less stereotyped.

Demonstrating causal influences of television on sex stereotypes is difficult because such stereotypes abound throughout the society, not just on television. One method is the natural experiment. Williams (1986) and her colleagues studied three communities in British Columbia. At the first time of measurement, one did not have access to television, but the other two did. The introduction of television into the unexposed community increased sex stereotyping among children (Kimball, 1986).

Two longitudinal studies of early adolescents also provide a stronger case than correlational studies for causal effects of television viewing on gender-role attitudes and beliefs. Both studies are based on Gerbner's cultivation hypothesis, which contains the assumption that television conveys a uniform set of sexist messages; hence, the more people are exposed, the more stereotyped messages they are likely to receive. In a two-year panel study of sixth through tenth graders, Morgan (1982) examined the association between television viewing and attitudes toward women in the workplace. For girls, the amount of television viewed predicted sexism scores a year later; for boys, however, sexist attitudes predicted the television viewed a year later. Using a similar design,

Morgan (1987) assessed attitudes toward household chores, household chores actually done, and amount of nightly television exposure for eighth graders. For both boys and girls, heavy television viewing predicted a later tendency to endorse traditional sex-role divisions of labor with respect to household chores. Although television viewing did not predict the sex-typing of chores actually done, heavy viewers did show increases in the congruence between their attitudes and their behaviors. Taken together, these studies suggest that exposure to the predominant messages on television, which are highly stereotyped, increases adolescents' sex-stereotyped beliefs and attitudes.

The most direct evidence of the effects of television on children's sex roles are studies specifically designed to change traditional stereotypes through the use of television (Durkin, 1985c). Calvert and Huston (1987) noted the difficulty in getting young children to perceive counter-stereotypical material and the distortions that may occur as a result of existing gender concepts. Nevertheless, efforts to change gender-role behavior, when correctly executed, do have some positive effects. For example, evaluations of *Freestyle,* a television series designed to reduce sex-stereotyped career interests, demonstrated that it changed stereotypes and attitudes among children shown the program in school (Johnston & Ettema, 1982). Moreover, early adolescent girls studied in 1986 expressed high aspirations and positive attitudes about female participation in traditionally masculine occupations (e.g., that of lawyer) in which women were frequently portrayed on television. They less often aspired to traditionally feminine and masculine occupations not shown on television (Wroblewski & Huston, 1987).

If television can modify sex-role concepts, there is every reason to assume that it plays a significant role in the initial formation of stereotypes as well. The theoretical mechanisms by which this occurs are not well understood, however (Katz, 1979). Calvert and Huston (1987) discuss the importance of gender-schema formation; Feshbach et al. (1979) highlight the importance of observational and incidental learning; and Greenberg (1988) proposes the drench effect to complement the gradual accretion of images and beliefs implied by the cultivation theory.

GAYS AND LESBIANS

Some interesting parallels between portrayals of gays and lesbians and portrayals of women and ethnic minorities can be found, but there are important differences as well. Much of the analysis of gay and lesbian portrayals is qualitative rather than quantitative. Nevertheless, the trend from nonrecognition to nonrespect is evident. Until the mid-1960s, homosexuals were almost never portrayed on television, paralleling the experience of most minorities. When interest began to be expressed, there was a period in which homosexuality was associated with mental illness and suicide, stressing its negative implications. Increased media exposure occurred primarily for male homosexuals; lesbians were relatively invisible, paralleling the general trends of female versus male portrayals (Altman, 1982).

According to some authors, television has been more honest on this issue than movies have been, particularly since the 1970s. In 1973 the Gay Activist Alliance and National Gay Task Force put out a series of guidelines about making scapegoats of gays and lesbians in the media, which television has followed for the most part. Insulting and demeaning names and derogatory humor have been largely absent in recent years. In the 1970s, gays began to be portrayed in a more balanced and prolific way on television than in films (cf. Chesebro, 1981; Galloway, 1983; Russo, 1981). One American television milestone was *That Certain Summer* (airing in 1972), a story of a gay man (played by Hal Holbrook) who confronts his son with the issue. By the mid-1970's, gay and lesbian characters appeared on almost every situation comedy, drama, and talk show on prime-time television. A 1976 dramatization of Walt Whitman's life by CBS is highly regarded by gay researchers as one of the earliest honest presentations of a gay hero. A British television show, *The Naked Civil Servant*, was based on the true story of an effeminate male homosexual, who turned out to be a popular character with viewers in both England and the United States.

A book edited by Galloway in 1983 traces the role of gay portrayals in movies and television in Britain. Despite the proliferation of gay characters, one of the authors concludes, "Life as most gay people know it is only vaguely approximated by any of the media. . . . They [the media] retain a very narrow definition of human behavior." This point was also made in a study in which Chesebro (1981) examined English audience reactions to the show *Barney Miller* (an American situation comedy, about a police station house, that frequently featured homosexuals). He found that homosexual audiences were considerably more inclined to find stereotypes in the program than were heterosexual groups (although both liked the program). The majority of the heterosexual community assessed was not aware of any actual contact with homosexuals during their daily routine. Those with contact, however, were more inclined to perceive stereotypes than those without it. This research shows an interesting parallel to the studies on ethnic minorities: for many people, most of their contact with and information about gays and lesbians is derived from media presentations.

Most of the available analyses antedated the current concern with AIDS, which has undoubtedly affected people's perceptions of homosexuals. Wober (1987) evaluated a British broadcast campaign on AIDS. Tolerance towards homosexuals increased, and support for coercive measures decreased in proportion to the number of these programs seen. Although there was also an attempt to change sexual behavior through these programs (namely, the use of condoms and the reduction in the number of sexual partners), such behavior did not seem to be affected in those who watched the programs. It appears that considerably more research is needed, particularly within this country, before we can say much about current appraisals. It is clear that the picture did improve through the beginning of the 1980's, but it is important to assess how things have changed as a result of AIDS.

SUMMARY AND IMPLICATIONS

Both Gerbner's cultural indicators model and Clark's model of legitimacy suggest that the number and types of portrayals of a social group symbolize its importance, power, and social value. Each of the five groups discussed—children, elderly people, minorities, women, and gays and lesbians—are often underrepresented or portrayed in narrow, stereotyped roles on television. Their low social status and relatively low value as a market for advertising both probably contribute to these patterns of television portrayals. Changes in the frequency of representation and in the types of roles portrayed occurred for blacks in the 1960s and 1970s and for women, gays, and lesbians in the 1970s and 1980s. Such changes are to some degree responses to political and social concerns of the day and, as a result, may not be lasting. Representation of blacks declined after the black power movement lost influence, and portrayals of women dropped after a peak in the mid-1980s.

Despite extensive documentation of television content, there is relatively little solid evidence about the effects of television portrayals on self-images, or on the perceptions, attitudes, or behavior of other groups. In the domain of sex stereotypes, however, the evidence that points to the powerful influence of television is relatively strong. There is every reason to believe that similar processes apply to other types of social images. One reason for the scarcity of evidence may be the difficulty in isolating the effects of television from those of other social and cultural sources. In this sense, television does reflect many of the realities of American society.

Planned programming that is designed to produce positive images of various subgroups has generally been successful. Sex stereotypes about careers, intergroup attitudes, and attitudes about elderly people can be affected by planned programs. The studies about such programs serve two purposes. They demonstrate that television portrayals do have effects, and they suggest a direction for improving programming.

Such popular entertainment programs as *The Cosby Show* and *Golden Girls* also present different images than those that are typical of earlier programming. Although these programs may be a relatively small proportion of what is available, their impact may be substantial because their characters are highly salient (Greenberg, 1988).

Despite the intense concern of many citizens about the effects of television images, the research agenda remains wide open for examining the effects of television's portrayals on self-perceptions, and intergroup attitudes, aspirations, and behaviors. Does television stimulate prejudice or diminish minority-group self-esteem? Does it limit or expand the self-perceptions of girls and boys? Does the lack of reality affect people's conceptions about the lives and problems of the elderly, women, or other groups? Do children, adolescents, and adults respond differently to television images? What specific behaviors are affected by television portrayals? In order to answer these questions, psychologists and other behavioral scientists need to develop appropriate research models that address the context in which television is presented, within- and between-subject differences, and the web of interactions that make meaningful television research difficult.

Although our knowledge is incomplete, psychologists and other professionals in human behavior can use research findings to assist television programmers in understanding what types of portrayals may have positive or negative effects on viewers. This technical assistance from outside the industry could eliminate much of the trial and error that typifies television's incorporation of inter-ethnic, cross-racial themes, gay and lesbian themes, and gender roles.

Emotions and Social Behavior

Television portrays social interactions and relationships, ranging from family interactions to relations with strangers in strange places. People express feelings, empathy, kindness, and sexuality; they also demonstrate cruelty, insensitivity, and violence. In this chapter, we discuss these images and their influences in four domains: family relationships, emotions, sexuality, and violence.

The impact of television images on individual viewers and on society as a whole has been conceptualized in several theoretical frameworks. Gerbner's cultural indicators model suggests that television contains a common set of themes about appropriate and inappropriate social relations and behaviors that reflect cultural values and that cultivate the belief that the patterns shown are normative. Because television contains a consistent set of messages, heavy viewers from varied social backgrounds come to share a common set of beliefs, a process described as *mainstreaming*. They live in the mainstream of the television world. People are also especially likely to respond to themes and messages that are congruent with their everyday experience or are perceived as highly realistic, a process described as *resonance*. When television resonates with real life, its messages have a double impact (Gerbner, Gross, Morgan, & Signorielli, 1980; Hawkins & Pingree, 1982).

Social-learning theory, with its cognitive elaborations (e.g., Bandura, 1977; Berkowitz, 1984; Berkowitz & Rogers, 1986; Stein & Friedrich, 1975), has guided a great deal of research on social behavior. According to that theory, televised social behavior serves as a model that is learned through observation. The viewer incorporates television messages into a cognitive framework or a set of schemata. Hence, individuals recall or learn what they can assimilate into existing schemata. Much of what is learned by observation can influence a person's beliefs and expectations about the world, even if it is never imitated. Some of what is learned will be translated into behavior; some of the factors that influence what is imitated include vicarious reinforcement and punishment, perceived utility, and individual abilities.

Arousal is a third process proposed to account for the influences of televised messages about emotion, sexuality, and violence (Zillmann, 1982). According to arousal theory, such messages can lead to nonspecific physiological and cognitive arousal that will in turn energize a wide range of potential behaviors. Arousal in one context may transfer to a subsequent viewing experience as well as to other forms of behavior. One important implication of the arousal theory is that a television program may activate behavior that is quite different in content and form from what is shown on the screen. For instance, sexual portrayals can stimulate violence if there are personality or environmental cues that predispose a person to act violently.

We have not tried to evaluate these theories systematically in every section of this chapter; rather, hypotheses based on each theory are discussed as needed to interpret the available literature. We specifically emphasize both the positive and the negative effects of television in this discussion, with a particular effort to highlight areas of influence that have not been discussed extensively in earlier literature. Historically, research and commentary has concentrated heavily on the effects of violence, leading to a relative neglect of other potentially important domains of social behavior and emotion. For that reason, we give more attention to studies of family relations, emotion, and sexuality, and consider those about violence only briefly.

FAMILY RELATIONSHIPS

The structure of American families has altered dramatically over the past 30 to 40 years. These changes include a shift from a predominance during the late 1940s and early 1950s of nuclear families comprising a mother, a father, and several children to a highly varied collection of nuclear families with one or two children, single parent households (predominantly female-headed), reconstituted or blended families following divorce and remarriage, and married or unmarried couples who prefer to remain childless (Freedman, 1988; Thomas & Callahan, 1982).

Does television programming mirror this diversity of family structures? Do particular programs resonate for a viewer because they speak to the concerns and experiences of the viewer's family structure? And do the portrayals of families on television influence the public's perception of the typical family?

Families on the Small Screen

Analyses of family portrayals document changes from the 1950s to the 1980s that mirror the real world in some respects, but distort or fail to represent it in other respects (Greenberg, Buerkel-Rothfuss, Neuendorf, & Atkin, 1980). In an analysis of family portrayals from 1946 through 1978, Glennon and Butsch (1982) concluded that such portrayals show a contrast between working-class and middle-class families. In the 1950s, middle-class families had idealized superfathers who were omniscient and omnipotent (e.g., *Father Knows Best*). In working-class families, fathers tended to be buffoons (e.g., *Life of Riley*). By the 1970s, working-class parents were portrayed in more positive and competent roles, but the children in such families were often upwardly mobile (e.g., *The Waltons, Good Times*); hence, the portrayals did not necessarily show esteem for a working-class lifestyle (Butsch & Glennon, 1980). Middle-class families continued to be perfect, but were more psychologically complex than their earlier counterparts. Mothers shifted from being background characters to being active members of families. Families displayed a range of conflict-resolution patterns, but were generally harmonious (Skill, Wallace, & Cassata, 1990).

Taylor (1987; Taylor & Walsh, 1987) proposes that television portrayals of families have supported the status quo by denying or disregarding many of the changes occurring in society. She suggests that the television programming of the 1950s and 1960s affirmed the view of a cozy nuclear family composed of mother, father, and two or three children interacting in a warm, loving, comfortable relationship in which there are no major problems, or at least no problems that cannot be solved in 30 or 60 minutes. We need only cast our minds back to the Nelsons of *Ozzie and Harriet* or the Andersons of *Father Knows Best* to draw up images of this era. In the 1950s, major changes in real-world families were occurring, beginning with an increase in early marriages, coupled with an increase in divorce. Birth rates increased until 1957, then family size began to decline. Such shows as *Leave it to Beaver* were affirming a view of the family that was not tied to the experiences of most Americans. What these shows produced was "not the reality of most family lives, but a post-war ideology, breezily forecasting a steady rate of economic growth that would produce sufficient abundance to eliminate the basis for class and ethnic conflict" (Taylor, 1987, p.6).

These hypotheses are partly supported by a review of the portrayals of families from 1947 to 1987 (Murray, 1990). In Table 3.1 (p. 59), 40 years' worth of television shows depicting families are listed. Examination of the range and frequency of these various family structures confirms the impression that there were shifts in the portrayal of families on television during those years.

Programs in the late 1940s and early 1950s were characterized by two family patterns. The first consisted of a mother, father, and two or three children. The second was a childless couple, newly wed, and struggling with the complications of their new status. By the late 1950s, couples with children predominated.

Television families have mirrored other changes in society, but television tends to follow social change cautiously rather than leading it. In the 1960s, reconstituted or blended families began to appear. For example, in *The Brady Bunch*, a widow and widower combined their two families. Single-parent families also appeared, though they were unusual in many respects. In almost all cases, the original family disruption resulted from parental death rather than divorce, a pattern that did not represent the real-world probabilities. Even more striking, many single-parent families were headed by men, a phenomenon that remained strong through the 1960s and occurred in about 30 series with widely differing themes. The most dramatic instance of the male-headed household was *Bonanza,* in which three sons of one man were all born to different mothers. Each mother was killed off in the series shortly after the birth of her son. The first mother died in childbirth, the second was killed in an Indian raid, and the third died when she was thrown from her horse not long after the birth. *Bonanza* was joined by programs as diverse as *Bachelor Father, Circus Boy, Bonino, My Three Sons, Kentucky Jones,* and *Sky King.* This trend continued into the 1970s, with series such as *Paper Moon* and *The Cop and the Kid,* and the 1980s, with *Emerald Point NAS,* but it was most striking in the 1960s. What is most peculiar about this male-headed-household phenomenon is that it bears no relationship to what was occurring in the real world. Throughout the 1960s, 1970s, and 1980s, about 90% of single-parent families were headed by mothers; fewer than 10% were headed by fathers (Garfinkel & McLanahan, 1986).

In the 1980s, there was a mixture of programs, some of which showed the struggles of divorced, female parents, as in *Kate and Allie,* and others that returned to the mom and dad and children family structures, as in *The Cosby Show* and *Family Ties.* Mothers in 1980s series usually had jobs, but both parents seemed to have plenty of time to deal with the needs and concerns of their children. Issues of poverty, child care, role overload, child support, and other important concerns of real-world families rarely entered the lives of these television families.

Effects on Viewers

Family comedies are popular with children and adults. One would expect that viewers' images and attitudes about family life would be affected by television, but little information exists about the effects of viewing (cf. Bryant, 1990; Gantz, 1985; Gunter & Svennevig, 1987; McLeod, Fitzpatrick, Glynn, & Fallis, 1982). Do children learn about family interactions from television? Do parents learn parenting techniques (Buerkel-Rothfuss, Greenberg, Atkin, & Neuendorf, 1982)? In one investigation, children were asked to evaluate the realism of television families and to judge the similarity of television families to their own families. Children judged traditional families (those with two natural parents and a homemaker mother) as more realistic and ideal than nontraditional television families, despite the fact that many of the children themselves lived in nontraditional families. One reason might be that intact families are portrayed as more harmonious than nonintact families (Skill et al., 1990). The apparent socioeconomic status of the television families was not related to children's judgments about realism (Dorr, Kovaric, & Doubleday, 1990). Children apparently incorporate the image of the traditional family as the norm, even with the many changes in society and on television.

Families are central to many of the most popular programs on television, but data on the effects of family portrayals are scant at best. New research is needed to investigate what children and adults learn from different family portrayals and to determine how they relate that knowledge to their own family experiences. Seeing affectionate and adequate parenting on television may help children to survive and overcome a dysfunctional family; it might help parents as well. Conversely, seeing unrealistically happy and united families on television might create dissatisfaction and disharmony. A healthy family life is critical to children and to many adults; we should place a high priority on gaining more knowledge about how television does and can contribute to it.

AFFECT AND EMOTION

Television comedy, drama, and even news can stimulate intense emotion, and it can teach viewers about emotion (Dorr, 1982). A person's emotional state can also influence what is viewed and how it is interpreted. The literature on television and emotion can be divided into four areas: (1) the influence of the viewer's affective state on viewing behavior, (2) the affective content of television programming, (3) effects on viewers' cognitions and beliefs about affect, and (4) effects on viewers' affective states.

Influence of Affective State on Viewing
In the uses and gratifications approach to studying television viewing (Blumler & Katz, 1974; Rosengren, Wenner, & Palmgreen,

1985), children and adults have been surveyed to learn why, in general, they watch television (cf. Greenberg, 1974; Katz, Gurevitch, & Haas, 1973; Kippax & Murray, 1980), the varieties of programs or genres watched (cf. Bantz, 1982; Kovaric, 1987), and the individual series or programs watched (cf. Wenner, 1985). In most research, people report that the act of viewing television is motivated by both cognitive and affective concerns.

Affective motivations include the desire for increased pleasurable arousal and the desire for decreased noxious arousal. People say they want to see something exciting or thrilling, to escape boredom, or to take their minds off their problems. Various researchers, most notably Zillmann and his associates, have attempted to determine experimentally the extent to which such arousal-related motivations actually determine viewing choices (cf. Zillmann, 1985). For instance, Bryant and Zillmann (1984) found that, given the choice, bored adult subjects will choose exciting television programs more often than relaxing programs, whereas stressed subjects will choose the reverse. However, highly stressed subjects seem more likely to avoid television altogether (Christ & Medoff, 1984; Medoff, 1980). Similar results have been found with children. Masters, Ford, and Arend (1983) found that 4- and 5-year-old boys placed in a hostile social environment viewed more nurturing television (*Mister Rogers' Neighborhood*) than those placed in a nurturing or neutral environment.

People often select programs that fit their affective state (Wakshlag, Vial, & Tamborini, 1983). Adults who demonstrated concern and sympathy for others were more apt to view the *Jerry Lewis Muscular Dystrophy Telethon* than less sympathetic people (Davis, 1983). However, in an examination of subjects' preferences for comedy while in negative affective states, Meadowcroft and Zillmann (1987) found that menstrual and premenstrual women preferred comedy over other programming choices more than did women midway through their cycles. Provoked subjects also avoided "hostile" comedy programming. Frustrated subjects preferred such comedy, and neither frustrated nor provoked subjects avoided nonhostile comedy (Medoff, 1980; Zillmann, Hezel, & Medoff, 1980).

Although there is a sizable body of descriptive research about affective gratifications, little is known about the processes involved. For instance, television as a medium, or particular programs or characters, may become such an object of attachment for some children that they are distressed by its absence and comforted by its presence. Although selective-exposure studies have demonstrated that one's affective state influences viewing choices, the role of unverbalized and unconscious motives versus conscious motivations has barely begun to be explored. Moreover, there are only a few studies that include viewer motivation as a predictor variable.

Affective Content in Television Programming
Television constantly portrays people experiencing and expressing joy, sorrow, excitement, fear, surprise, anger, guilt, and disgust. The consequences of such emotions are regularly depicted. Because affect is central to mental health, we need a systematic description of the affective content of television if we are to understand its possible roles in the emotional development of the child. Content analyses could describe how much of what kinds of emotion are depicted, the situations in which people typically experience or express emotions, the consequences for such expressions, and the social rules for emotional expression. At a more abstract level, one could identify the theoretical models of emotional experience that television programming implicitly presents.

Yet, content analysis of emotions is rare. In one study, the affective content of six types of programming (situation comedies, mystery and suspense series, general dramas, cartoons, children's educational programming, and programming featuring families) was described (Dorr, Doubleday, & Kovaric, 1983; Kovaric, Doubleday, & Dorr, in preparation). Anger, fear, interest or excitement, joy, and sadness typically occurred more frequently than guilt, amusement, or disgust. Situation comedies featured the most anger; mystery and suspense series dwelled most heavily on fear; children's educational programs and mystery and suspense series contained the most interest or excitement; and joy figured most prominently in children's educational programming and in general drama. Cartoons were consistently worse than other genres in portraying characters who managed well following positive or negative emotions, in the extent to which verbal and nonverbal emotional expression corresponded, and in the centrality of emotion to family interactions.

Effects on Cognitions and Beliefs About Affect

Because television programming contains abundant information about affect, viewers may learn to recognize emotional displays, acquire beliefs about how often people experience different emotions, understand that certain situations are associated with certain affective states, accept social expectations regarding emotional expression and behavior, and come to believe in certain models of emotional responsiveness, experience, expression, and behavior (Doubleday, Kovaric, Dorr, & Beizer-Seidner, 1986).

Children recognize some televised emotions at an early age. Preschoolers accurately identified pleasure and annoyance displayed by videotaped actors (Deutsch, 1974), and 7-year-olds almost always accurately labeled happiness and sadness of same-aged children presented in slides. They labeled anger correctly 50% of the time, and fear about 20% of the time (Feshbach & Roe, 1968). Children did not readily attend to or understand filmed or televised symbolic emotion, although, of course, older children typically did so more than younger children, especially when the symbolism involved romance (Garry, 1970; Keilhacker, 1969).

Planned programming can promote children's understanding of feelings. Preschoolers who were regular viewers of *Sesame Street* learned more about the emotions preschoolers typically feel in a variety of situations than did infrequent viewers (Bogatz & Ball, 1971).

Effects on Viewers' Affective States

Viewers (primarily children) manifest a wide variety of emotions in response to television—happiness, interest, involvement, excitement, anger, disgust, fear, sadness, and surprise (e.g., Ekman, et al., 1972; Eyre-Brook, 1972; Filipson, Schyller, & Hoijer, 1974;

Garry, 1970; Lesser, 1974; Linne, 1971; Zillmann, Weaver, Mundorf, & Aust, 1986). Although there is great variability in such experiences, even to a single program, these responses can persist for up to a period of weeks (Eyre-Brook, 1972; Sturm, 1975, 1978).

Effects on physiological arousal have been demonstrated. Children exhibit increasingly strong physiological responses to filmed love scenes with increasing age (Dysinger & Ruckmick, 1933). Levi (1965) found increases in adults' adrenalin and noradrenalin levels when exposed to humorous, violent, and horrifying films, though Carruthers and Taggert (1973) did not find such differences.

Television can also decrease arousal (Wadeson, Mason, Hamburg, & Handlon, 1963). Exposure to television fare that involved adult subjects in programming not related to their affective state (annoyed) led to decreased arousal (Bryant & Zillmann, 1977). In fact, adults reported relaxation and passivity as predominant moods during television viewing (Kubey & Csikszentmihalyi, 1990).

Repeated exposure to arousing content or form on television can lead to desensitization, a process that can be helpful for reducing fear. Children showed reduced fear of dogs after exposure to a model exhibiting nonanxious interactions with dogs (Bandura & Menlove, 1968). Children facing surgery were less anxious after seeing a film depicting a child facing an operation than after viewing a control film (Melamed & Siegel, 1975).

It is often asserted in the popular press that television viewing results in a passive, "zombie-like" mental state on the part of the viewers. These articles usually cite Krugman's (1971) study of EEG responses of one subject to three advertisements. The EEGs showed a preponderance of delta and theta waves, which usually occur during sleep. A more systematic study of 56 subjects exposed to a variety of half-hour and hour programming demonstrated no support for the assertion; brainwave patterns during viewing (predominantly beta) were typical of most waking activities (Miller, 1985).

Cognitive developmental changes influence children's affective responses to television. The strength and content of children's fearful reactions change with age, presumably because of changes in what they understand about the content being presented. Young children react with greater fear to films and television than older children, and they often enjoy scary programs less (Cantor & Reilly, 1982; Palmer, Hockett, & Dean, 1983). Children younger than about 7 tend to report being frightened by things that look scary even though they are highly improbable. One example is the physical transformation of the main character in *The Incredible Hulk*. The reason for their fear appears to be preoperational failure to grasp conservation of matter firmly; changes in appearance are interpreted as changes in identity.

In middle childhood, children develop a greater capacity to evaluate the likelihood and reality of what they see. They tend to be frightened by material that is possible or realistic (Cantor & Sparks, 1984; Sparks, 1986; Sparks & Cantor, 1986). Parents reported that children in this age group were especially frightened by the film *The Day After*, which depicted the aftereffects of a nuclear war (Cantor, Wilson, & Hoffner, 1986). Fearful reactions to another program were reduced for this age group when they were told it was not real or were instructed to take the role of an endangered character (Cantor & Wilson, 1984). Interestingly, describing potentially frightening scenes to adults before they viewed them resulted in increased fear responses, with the more explicit descriptions resulting in the greater fear responses (Cantor, Ziemke, & Sparks, 1984).

Empathy with characters can increase emotional responses in both children and adults. Adults reported feeling stress corresponding to the experimentally varied amounts depicted in a film; those scoring higher on an identification scale experienced more stress (Wilson & Cantor, 1985). For adults, empathetic identification is apparently enhanced if the material preceding the current segment being viewed is of the same emotional tone (positive or negative), is arousing, and there is enough time between segments to allow for cognitive reorientation (Zillmann, Mody, & Cantor, 1974).

Viewers who are more predisposed to be empathic are also more apt to share in the emotions they see on television. Preschool children identified less with a television character's fear than did 9- to 11-year-old children. Although the younger children recognized that the character was fearful almost as well as the older children, they had less ability to take the perspective of that character (Wilson & Cantor, 1985). Adult viewers are most apt to share in characters' emotions when they are predisposed to take other people's point of view and when they are induced to role-take before viewing (Davis, Hull, Young, & Warren, 1987).

Clearly, research in the domain of television and affect has been concentrated on television's emotional effects on viewers. Still, there are gaps here, too. With the notable exception of Cantor's programmatic studies of children's fear, there is little work that takes an explicitly developmental perspective. And although fear may legitimately occupy the center of this research stage, few would assert that overall emotional well-being is tied primarily to fear. Thus, greater attention ought to be paid to other emotional responses to television, including joy, sadness, interest and excitement, anger, guilt, and more complex emotions, with particular attention to developmental changes that may affect these responses.

When television content viewed by children conveys subtle affective responses, the child's own emotional repertoire may develop. On the other hand, when programming depicts crude and uncontrolled emotional displays, the child's affective growth may be negatively affected (see Feshbach, 1988).

SEXUALITY

A 1987 Louis Harris poll of American adults indicated that more than two thirds of those surveyed were concerned in general about the impact of television on the values and behaviors of their children. Two thirds believed that television encourages teenagers to be sexually active and does not portray sexuality in a realistic manner. With increasing debates on abortion, contraception, AIDS, and pornography, the question of the influence of sexual content on television will continue to be at the forefront of public debate.

Most people assume that television is an educator about sexuality for children. In her review of the literature for the National Institute of Mental Health report *Television and Behavior,* Roberts (1982) noted four attributes of television that would make this medium a prime contributor to a child's sexual socialization. First, the programs dealing with sexuality are not intended for viewing by children. This is even more true of cable programs and videotapes than of broadcast television. Second, children have access to few alternative sources of information about sexuality because parents and schools often provide little or no sex education. Moreover, because most sexual activity is carried out in private, children have few opportunities for direct observation. Third, television tends to portray issues of sex in a realistic manner, promoting easy social and emotional identification by the child. And finally, the messages about sexuality on television are consistent, creating the conditions for maximum impact.

Sex on Commercial Television

Explicit sex is not often shown on broadcast television. Content analyses conducted in the late 1970s and early 1980s showed that sexual acts were suggested rather than shown, and they occurred very infrequently in relation to acts of violence (e.g., Cantor & Cantor, 1984; Greenberg & D'Alessio, 1985; Silverman, Sprafkin, & Rubinstein, 1979; Sprafkin & Silverman, 1981). Nonetheless, certain messages about sex were often conveyed. Implied sexual activity occurred most often between unmarried couples who had little emotional attachment or commitment to one another. Although contraception was almost never discussed or implied, pregnancy and sexually transmitted diseases rarely resulted. There is some evidence that commercial television has been changing since the 1970s, with increasingly frequent and explicit images and messages about sex (Haffner & Kelly, 1987). In this area, as in others, ongoing content analyses are needed.

Because sexuality is such a socially sensitive topic, little research that investigates the impact of television on children's sexual learning, per se, is available. In one investigation, Peterson, Moore, and

Furstenburg (1984) queried children about their exposure to television programs containing sexual content, once in 1976 when the children were 10 to 11 years old and then again five years later when the same children were about 16. At Time 2, the adolescents were asked about their sexual experience. There were no statistically significant relations between exposure to televised sexual content at age 10 and sexual behavior at age 16. In another experiment, high school students were randomly assigned to view excerpts of television entertainment programs depicting (1) prostitution, (2) married intercourse, (3) unmarried intercourse, or (4) homosexuality. Exposure to all but unmarried intercourse increased students' understanding of sexual terms (e.g., "solicitation," "coming on to someone," and "getting in a family way"). None of the excerpts affected expressed beliefs and values about sexual activities, e.g., the rightness or wrongness of prostitution, unmarried intercourse, and homosexuality.

These experimental investigations were concerned with the implicit and indirect portrayals of sexuality that are typical of broadcast television. They suggest that exposure to such images has a limited effect. Increased knowledge about sexual terminology may occur, but there is no evidence that changes in beliefs, attitudes, and values regarding sexual practices take place. Nor is there evidence that changes in sexual behavior occur. There are no experimental studies, however, in which children or adolescents have been exposed to the explicit sexual depictions that often occur on pay-cable channels, so many questions remain about the impact of televised sexuality.

Adolescents may resist the influence of messages on entertainment television when they perceive them as unrealistic and different from real life. In a recent investigation, about two thirds of a sample of students in eighth, tenth, and twelfth grades said they used television as one source of sexual information; however, they rated it least helpful of 10 possible sources. When asked a series of questions about the likelihood of sexual events on television and in real life, they differentiated between the two contexts. They responded that sexual behavior among unmarried and uncommitted partners is more common on television than in real life, that birth control is used less frequently on television than in real life, and that negative consequences of sexual behavior (i.e., pregnancy and disease) are less likely on television than in real life (Truglio, 1990).

Although the data on adolescents are sparse (Greenberg, Linsangan, Soderman, & Heeter, 1988), studies of college students and young adults suggest that explicit sexual content, particularly messages about sexual violence, has a strong impact. Films about rape and aggression against women often promote the rape myth— that female victims really want to be overcome or that they derive pleasure from being assaulted. While the vast majority of this research (e.g., Malamuth & Briere, 1986; Donnerstein, Linz, & Penrod, 1987) has been concerned with films that would not be shown on commercial television, a number of studies have included sexually violent materials that would be shown on prime time. In general, this research suggests that exposure to sexual violence can indirectly contribute to antisocial behavior via the reinforcement of certain attitudes, perceptions, and beliefs about violence against women.

Sex on Cable Television and Videotapes
Although broadcast television usually portrays suggestive, nonviolent, and nonvisual images of sex, cable channels and videotapes contain explicit visual and sometimes violent sexuality. Both R- and X-rated materials are readily available in most communities (with X-rated materials mainly on videotapes). Available research certainly indicates that viewing the sexual violence available on cable and videotape can lead to antisocial consequences (Linz, Donnerstein, & Penrod, 1987a, 1987b; Malamuth & Donnerstein, 1982).

In discussing sexually violent cable and videotape materials and their impact, it is useful to group them in five categories. This typology includes materials that would not be considered obscene or pornographic in a legal sense. Likewise, it does not completely classify the materials into mutually exclusive categories, but it represents subdivisions that appear to have different effects on viewers. It is important to keep in mind that the research discussed is limited to adult viewers (17 years of age or older).

1. *Erotica* refers to materials that could be R- or X-rated, with implied or actual sexual contact. There is no violent or degrading content, and any form of coercion, psychological or otherwise, is nonexistent. Materials of this nature are available on both cable television (primarily pay movie channels) and videotapes. Current research indicates that there are no antisocial effects from exposure to such images (Donnerstein et al., 1987).

2. *Nonviolent sexually explicit materials that are degrading to women* have in common the debasing depiction of women as willing recipients of any male sexual urge (excluding rape) or as oversexed, highly promiscuous individuals with insatiable sexual urges. The material is X-rated and available only in the videotape market or on specialized pay cable channels. With regard to the effects of this material, the research is inconsistent. Some studies of long-term exposure have found negative effects on attitudes and perceptions about women for both male and female viewers (e.g., Zillmann & Bryant, 1984), whereas other studies (the majority) have found no effects.

3. *Violent pornography* depicts sexual coercion in a sexually explicit context. Usually a man uses force against a woman in order to obtain sexual gratification. A common theme of many of these depictions is the "positive-victim outcome," in which rape and other forms of sexual assault are shown as pleasurable and sexually arousing to the female victim. Pleasure for the victim is an obvious contrast to other forms of media violence. This material is X-rated and available only in the videotape market. Men exposed to this material can become sexually aroused, they report calloused attitudes about rape, and in laboratory studies they increase their aggression against women. Current research indicates that these attitude and arousal patterns may have some relationship to real-world aggression toward women (e.g., Malamuth, 1986; Malamuth & Check, 1980). Two issues are important, however. The first is that these effects seem to occur most readily in those who already have certain calloused attitudes about rape. Second, they can occur without any sexual content in the

material. In other words, it is the violence or the message about violence that is important, not simply the sexual nature of the materials.

4. *Nonexplicit sexual aggression against women* includes depictions that are not sexually explicit (i.e., are not X-rated). There may be a rape scene, but it is often of the kind that would be permissible under television broadcast standards. While the material is not sexually explicit, the idea that women derive pleasure from sexual abuse is nonetheless a recurring theme. This material can be seen on commercial television as well as cable and videotape. Exposure to this type of content sometimes reinforces antisocial attitudes about rape, particularly in individuals with preexisting calloused rape-related attitudes.

5. *Sexualized violence against women* occurs in R-rated programs and films. Though less sexually explicit than X-rated materials, these films show far more graphic violence. They do not depict positive-victim outcomes, and the violence is not sexual violence (rape) but contains images of torture, murder, and mutilation in a sexual context. Pay-movie channels and videotapes are the main outlets. Recent studies (e.g., Donnerstein, et al., 1987) indicate that massive exposure to this type of material (4 to 10 hours) can lead to such desensitization effects as reduced emotional and physiological reactivity and reduced sensitivity to sexual violence (i.e., perceptions about a real rape victim). These effects seem to be similar for both men and women, although much more research is needed on women.

Effects on Children

The experimental research dealing with the effects of cable and videotaped sexual materials has been conducted with adults. For ethical reasons no one can conduct such studies on individuals under 17 years of age. However, there are good theoretical reasons (e.g., the learning of aggressive scripts) to expect that exposing children to messages endorsing sexual violence, even on commercial television, may eventually lead to the formation of antisocial attitudes and behaviors. In a recent report for the surgeon general of the United States (Mulvey & Haugaard, 1986), two possible outcomes from exposure to sexually explicit or violent materials were proposed. First, children in the 12- to 18-year-old range may show effects similar to those for adults. At this age children understand causation and the idea of reciprocity in relationships. However, they have fewer life experiences and some differences from adults in cognitive functioning that could lead to dissimilar effects. Second, for children under 12 there is the possibility of "imprinting," or teaching, early associations of sex with violence. On the other hand, there is the possibility of no effects because children of this age may have insufficient emotional or cognitive capacities to comprehend the message. Given the fact that many children now have access to strong sexual images on cable and videocassettes, there is no question that more research and discussion is needed regarding the potential impact of these materials on children.

VIOLENCE

The causes of violence in our society are many, the roots deep, and the possible solutions unclear. Some obvious causes of violence include growing up in an abusive family setting, or the experiences of frustration or hopelessness that stem from a chronic lack of economic resources or a long-continued denial of opportunity. However, the decision about whether or how we use violence in response to the many and varied conflicts that we all experience in our daily lives is also determined by the rules, norms, or standards of behavior that we observe in the world around us—the real world and the television world. Television plays a subtle role as a teacher of norms or standards of behavior, and learning from that teacher can occur during the seven hours per day that the television set is on in the typical household.

Debates about the effects of televised violence have been in the air throughout most of the 40 years of television's history. Official recognition of this problem began with congressional investigations in the mid-1950s and continued with the Commission on the Causes and Prevention of Violence (Baker & Ball, 1969), the Surgeon General's Scientific Advisory Committee on Television and Social Behavior (1972) and the update produced by the National Institute of Mental Health in 1982 (Pearl, Bouthilet, & Lazar, 1982). In 1985, the American Psychological Association took the position that television violence can cause aggressive behavior, after the Board on Social and Ethical Responsibility for Psychology surveyed the evidence on this topic (American Psychological Association, 1985).

Researchers have also devoted a great deal of attention to the issue. Since 1955, about 1,000 studies, reports, and commentaries concerning the impact of televised violence have been published (Eysenck & Nias, 1978; Liebert & Sprafkin, 1988; Murray, 1980; Murray & Kippax, 1978). Nevertheless, there is still some disagreement about how important television is as a causal agent in the real world (cf. Freedman, 1984, 1986; Friedrich-Cofer & Huston, 1986). In this discussion, we have not attempted to review all of the controversies or the literature, but to summarize some of the major points and to add recent data.

Television Content
Entertainment television includes large doses of televised violence. Indeed, as Figure 3.1 demonstrates, the results of almost two decades of content analyses conducted by a research team directed by George Gerbner and his associates (Gerbner & Gross, 1980; Gerbner, Gross, Eleey, Jackson-Beeck, Jeffries-Fox, & Signorielli, 1977, 1978; Gerbner, Gross, Morgan, & Signorielli, 1980, 1986; Gerbner & Signorielli, 1990) show that the level of violence in prime-time television has remained at about 5 violent acts per hour, while the level of violence in children's Saturday-morning programming is much higher, about 20 to 25 violent acts per hour. Since 1980, there have been dramatic increases in violence on children's television, with a peak of 30 to 32 violent acts per hour in 1981 and 1982.

The types of violence portrayed range from destruction of property to physical assaults that cause injury and death. If we multiply these rates of televised violence by the amount of viewing of the average preschooler and school-aged child (two to four hours per day), we begin to understand the magnitude of the problem. By

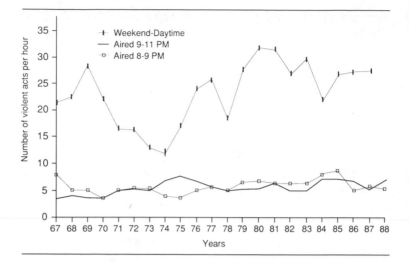

Figure 3.1. Rate of violent acts per hour for children's and prime-time programming from 1967 to 1988. From an unpublished manuscript by G. Gerbner and N. Signorielli, 1990, University of Pennsylvania, Annenberg School of Communications, Philadelphia, PA, Figure 2. Reprinted by permission of authors.

the time the average child graduates from elementary school, she or he will have witnessed at least 8,000 murders and more than 100,000 other assorted acts of violence. Depending on the amount of television viewed, our youngsters could see more than 200,000 violent acts before they hit the schools and streets of our nation as teenagers.

Relations between Viewing and Aggression

The accumulated research clearly demonstrates a correlation between viewing violence and aggressive behavior—that is, heavy viewers behave more aggressively than light viewers. Children and adults who watch a large number of aggressive programs also tend to hold attitudes and values that favor the use of aggression to resolve conflicts (Freedman, 1984; Liebert & Sprafkin, 1988). These correlations are solid. They remain even when many other potential influences on viewing and aggression are controlled, including education level, social class, aggressive attitudes, parental behavior, and sex-role identity (Belson, 1978; Huesmann, Lagerspetz, & Eron, 1984).

Causes

Both experimental and longitudinal studies support the hypothesis that viewing violence is causally associated with aggression. Studies conducted with preschoolers, school-aged children, college students, and adults confirm that viewing violence on television can lead to increases in aggressive attitudes, values, and behavior. The major initial experimental studies were conducted by Bandura and his colleagues with young children (Bandura, Ross, & Ross, 1961, 1963) and by Berkowitz and his associates with adolescents (Berkowitz, 1962; Berkowitz, Corwin, & Heironimus, 1963; Berkowitz & Rawlings, 1963; Geen & Rakowsky, 1973) in highly structured laboratory conditions. Subsequent studies used more typical television programs and more realistic measures of aggression, with similar results (e.g., Collins & Getz, 1976; Ellis & Sekyra, 1972; Frost & Stauffer, 1987; Geen, 1975; Liebert & Baron, 1972). It is clear from experimental studies that one can produce increased aggressive behavior as a result of either extended or brief exposure to televised violence, but such research does not determine whether heightened aggressiveness observed in the experimental setting spills over into daily life.

Natural Contexts

One means of investigating real-life effects is the field experiment in which the investigator presents typical television programs in the normal viewing setting and observes behavior where it naturally occurs. Field experiments with preschool children (Friedrich & Stein, 1973; Stein & Friedrich, 1972) and adolescents (Parke, Berkowitz, Leyens, West, & Sebastian, 1977) found heightened aggression among viewers assigned to watch violent television or films under some conditions (cf. Freedman, 1984; Friedrich-Cofer & Huston, 1986; Liebert & Sprafkin, 1988). One exception was Feshbach and Singer (1971). In a field experiment with adults, men who were asked to watch a diet of violent television were rated by their wives as more hurtful (for example, losing one's temper, shouting at the kids) than a group who watched a non-violent diet (Loye, Gorney, & Steele, 1977).

One unique source of information was provided in a natural experiment comparing children's aggressive behavior before and after television was introduced in their town (Joy, Kimball, & Zabrack, 1986; Williams, 1986). Children were compared with their peers in two other towns where television was well established. There were no differences among the three towns in the initial comparison, but two years later, the children from the former no-television town were significantly more aggressive, both physically and verbally, than the children in the other towns.

Longitudinal and cross-national studies also support the conclusion that viewing television violence leads to aggression that becomes a lasting part of individual behavior patterns. One group of individuals was studied at ages 8, 18, and 30. Viewing violence at age 8 predicted aggression at 18 for boys (Eron 1982, 1963; Eron, Lefkowitz, Huesmann, & Walder, 1972; Lefkowitz, Eron, Walder, & Huesmann, 1972) and serious criminal behavior at age 30 (Huesmann, Eron, Lefkowitz, & Walder, 1984). The most plausible interpretation of this finding is that a child's early preference for violent television programming and other media is one factor in the production of aggressive and antisocial behavior when that child becomes a young adult.

Parallel longitudinal studies were conducted in five countries: Australia, Finland, Israel, Poland, and the United States (Huesmann & Eron, 1986). Although the average levels of television violence in these other nations were much lower than those in the United States, the associations between viewing and aggression occurred in most populations studied. The analyses supported a bidirectional hypothesis—viewing violence leads to aggression, and aggressive tendencies lead to viewing violent television. The authors of another panel study concluded that their findings did not support a causal role for television violence in later aggressive behavior of boys (Milavsky, Kessler, Stipp, & Rubens, 1982), but methodological experts who examined their findings reversed that conclusion (Cook, Kendziersky, & Thomas, 1983).

Television violence can lead to desensitization as well as to aggressive behavior. Children and adults who are exposed to television violence show reduced physiological arousal, and they are less likely than unexposed individuals to seek help for victims of violence or to act on the behalf of victims (Cline, Croft, & Courrier, 1973; Drabman & Thomas, 1974; Thomas, 1982; Thomas, Horton, Lippincott, & Drabman, 1977).

Although there is continuing controversy about the interpretation of research evidence on the impact of television violence (e.g., Berkowitz, 1984; Freedman, 1984; Friedrich-Cofer & Huston, 1986; Liebert & Sprafkin, 1988; Murray, 1973, 1984; Murray & Kippax, 1978; National Institute of Mental Health, 1982; Pearl et al., 1982), most researchers would agree with the conclusion in a recent report by the National Institute of Mental Health (1982), that "violence on television does lead to aggressive behavior by children and teenagers who watch the programs. This conclusion is based on laboratory experiments and on field studies. Not all children become aggressive, of course, but the correlations between violence and aggression are positive. In magnitude, television violence is as strongly correlated with aggressive behavior as any other behavioral variable that has been measured. The research question has moved from asking whether or not there is an effect, to seeking explanations for the effect" (p.6). To this we would only add that the behavior patterns established in childhood and adolescence are the foundation for lifelong patterns manifested in adulthood.

SUMMARY

Television is a potentially powerful teacher about social relationships, intimacy, conflict, and feeling. Family relations, emotion, sexuality, and violence are the stuff of entertainment television. Although theory leads one to expect that viewers will absorb many of the messages about family relations, emotions, and sexual relationships that are presented on television, little research designed to assess that expectation has been conducted. Television is a subtle, continuous source for learning about the rules of life and society.

The family types portrayed on television have shifted over time, only partly reflecting changes in family structure in the society. In the early days of television, families fit the mold of two parents, a homemaker mother, and a few children. When single-parent families appeared, many of them were headed by fathers, and most were the result of the death of a parent rather than divorce. Content analyses provide relatively little information, however, about how family members interact, the types of parenting methods used, or the images of children and adolescents presented. Moreover, little is known about the effects of these portrayals. Children apparently consider families with a traditional structure to be more realistic, despite the fact that many families in 1990 depart from that structure.

Although we also know remarkably little about the nature of emotions displayed by television characters there is evidence of viewers' emotional responses. People use television to deal with their emotional states—seeking arousal when they are bored and seeking reduced arousal when they are under stress. Children also learn about emotions from television. They learn what situations lead to what emotions and the social norms for expressing emotion. People also respond emotionally to television content, but individual responses differ, depending on cognitive and personality characteristics.

Violence and sexuality are of particular social concern to citizens and professionals alike. American television contains a great deal of violence, a pattern that has been relatively stable over many years. Broadcast television contains little explicit sexuality, but does contain indirect, suggestive references to sexual behavior. Explicit sexuality is shown on cable television and commercially available videotapes. There is extensive evidence that television violence can influence aggressive attitudes and behavior. Sexually explicit material does not appear to induce antisocial behavior, except when it portrays sexual violence or violence in a sexual context. Adults respond to such material with increased callousness toward women and increased acceptance of rape and other forms of sexual violence.

Table 3.1 Programs Portraying Families on American
Television: 1947–1987

1947–51
Amos & Andy, Aldrich Family, Crime with Father, Detective's Wife, Egg
& I, Fairmeadows USA, First Hundred Years, George Burns and Gracie
Allen, The Goldbergs, I Love Lucy, I Remember Mama, Life of Riley,
Mixed Doubles, Mr. & Mrs. Mystery, Mr. & Mrs. North, One Man's
Family, Roy Rogers Show, Search for Tomorrow, Those Enduring Young
Charms, Wesley, Wren's Nest.

1952–56
Adventures of Ozzie & Harriet, As the World Turns, Bennets, Bonino,
Brave Eagle, Circus Boy, Claudia, Davy Crockett, December Bride, Ethel
& Albert, Father Knows Best, Fury, The Great Gildersleeve, Guiding
Light, Halls of Ivy, Heaven for Betsy, The Honeymooners, I Married
Joan, Imogene Coca Show, Jamie, Joe & Mabel, Lassie I, Life with Eliz-
abeth, Life with Father, Make Room for Daddy I, The Marriage, Meet
Corliss Archer, Mr. Adams & Eve, My Favorite Husband, My Friend
Flicka, My Little Margie, My Son Jeep, Norby, People's Choice, Portia
Faces Life, Pride of the Family, Professional Father, Road of Life, Secret
Storm, Sky King, Take It from Me, That's My Boy, Topper, Woman with
a Past.

1957–61
Andy Griffith, Angel, Bachelor Father, Bonanza, Buckskin, Casey Jones,
Date with the Angels, Dennis the Menace, Dick & the Duchess, Dick
Van Dyke Show, Donna Reed Show, Edy Wynn Show, Eve Arden Show,
Father of the Bride, Fibber McGee & Molly, Flintstones, From These
Roots, Guestward Ho, Harrigan & Son, The Hathaways, Hazel, Ichabod
and Me, Lucille Ball–Desi Arnez, Jefferson Drum, Laramie, Lassie II,
Leave It to Beaver, Love and Marriage, Lucy Show I, Make Room for
Daddy II, Margie, Mr. Ed, Mrs. G. Goes to College, My Three Sons,
National Velvet, One Happy Family, Peck's Bad Girl, Pete & Gladys,
Peter Loves Mary, The Real McCoys, The Rifleman, Thin Man, Today
Is Ours, The Tom Ewell Show, Too Young to Go Steady, Yes, Yes Nanette,
Young Doctor Malone.

Table 3.1 (Continued)

1962–66

Addams Family, Another World, Beverly Hillbillies, Bewitched, Big Valley, Bing Crosby, Cara Williams Show, Daktari, Daniel Boone, Dark Shadows, Days of Our Lives, Fair Exchange, Family Affair, Farmer's Daughter, Flipper, Gidget, Hank, I'm Dickens He's Fouster, Jean Arthur Show, The Jetsons, Joey Bishop Show, Kentucky Jones, Lassie III, Long Hot Summer, Lorretta Young Show, Lost in Space, Love on a Rooftop, Lucy Show II, Mickey, Mona McCluskey, The Monroes, Mr. Smith Goes to Washington, The Munsters, My Mother the Car, Ninety Bristol Court, Occasional Wife, O.K. Crackerly, Our Man Higgins, Paradise Bay, Patty Duke Show, Petticoat Junction, Pistols & Petticoats, Please Don't Eat the Daisies, The Pruitts of Southampton, Road West, Room for One More, Scarlet Hill, Travels of Jamie McPheeters, Wendy and Me, Young Marrieds.

1967–71

All in the Family, All My Children, Blondie, Brady Bunch, Courtship of Eddie's Father, Danny Thomas Show, Debbie Reynolds Show, Doris Day Show, Forsyte Saga, Gentle Ben, Ghost & Mrs. Muir, The Good Life, The Governor & JJ, Guns of Will Sonnett, He & She, Here's Lucy, High Chaparral, Jimmy Stewart Show, Julia, Lancer, Lassie IV, Love Is a Many Splendored Thing, McMillan & Wife, Amy Prentiss, Make Room for Granddaddy, Mayberry RFD, The Mothers-in-Law, My World and Welcome to It, Nancy, Nanny & the Professor, One Life to Live, The Partridge Family, Second Hundred Years, Skippy the Kangaroo, Smith Family, Somerset, The Survivors, That Girl, To Rome with Love, Trouble with Tracy, A World Apart.

1972–76

Adams Chronicles, Adventures of Black Beauty, Alice, Apple's Way, Beacon Hill, Big Eddie, Big John, Little John, Bob & Carol/Ted & Alice, Bob Crane Show, Bob Newhart Show, Born Free, Brady Kids, Bridget Loves Bernie, The Cop and the Kid, The Cowboys, Don Rickles, The Dumplings, A Family Affair, Family Holvak, Faraday & Co., Flintstone Comedy Hour, Girl with Something Extra, Good Times, Happy Days, Here We Go Again, How to Survive a Marriage, The Invisible Man, Ivan

Table 3.1 (Continued)

1972–76 (Continued)

the Terrible, The Jeffersons, Joe & Sons, Kate McShane, Kahn, KORG: 70,000 BC, Land of the Lost, Lassie V, Lassie VI, Little House on the Prairie, The Little People, Lotsa Luck, Love Thy Neighbor, Mary Hartman Mary Hartman, Maude, Me and the Chimp, The Montefuscos, Mr. T. & Tina, Muggsy, Nancy Walker Show, New Andy Griffith Show, New Land, No Honestly, One Day at a Time, Paper Moon, Partridge Family, Phyllis, Popi, The Practice, Return to Peyton Place, Rhoda, Rich Man Poor Man, Rockford Files, Roman Holidays, Ryan's Hope, Salty, Sanford & Son, Sigmund & the Sea Monster, The Snoop Sisters, Sons and Daughters, Sunshine, Swiss Family Robinson, Tenafly, The Texas Wheelers, That's My Mama, These Are the Days, Thicker than Water, Three for the Road, Toma, The Tony Randall Show, Touch of Grace, Upstairs Downstairs, Valley of the Dinosaurs, Viva Valdez, Wait Till Father Gets Home, The Waltons, We'll Get By, The Westwind, What's Happening, Who's the Boss, The Young and the Restless.

1977–81

American Dream, Angie I, II, III, Another Day, Another Life, Apple Pie, Archie Bunker's Place, Baby, I'm Back, Battlestar Galactica, The Baxters, Benson, Best of the West, Betty White Show, Beulah Land, Big Foot & Wild Boy, Big Hawaii, Big Shamus/Little Shamus, Billy, Black Beauty, Bless This House, Brady Brides, Breaking Away, Busting Loose, The Chisholms, Dallas, Days of Our Lives, Dear Detective, Diff'rent Strokes, Dukes of Hazzard, Dynasty, Eight Is Enough, Fall & Rise of Reginald Perrin, Father Dear Father, Faulty Towers, The Feather & Father Gang, The Fitzpatricks, Flambards, Flamingo Road, Fish, Flintstone Family Adventures, For Richer for Poorer, Forever Fernwood, Free Country, Gimme a Break, Good Neighbors, Grampa Goes to Washington, Hardy Boys Mystery, Harper Valley PTA, Harris & Co., Hart to Hart, Harvey Korman Show, Hello, Larry, Hizzoner, How the West Was Won, Husband & Wives, I'm a Big Girl Now, It's a Living, James at 15, Joe & Valerie, The Kallikaks, Kate Loves a Mystery, King of Kensington, Knots Landing, Ladies Man, Lanigan's Rabbi, The Lazarus Syndrome, Lewis & Clark, Life & Times of Eddie Roberts, Love Boat, Love Sidney, MacKenzies of Paradise Cove, Maggie, Makin' It, Married: The First Year, Me & Maxx,

Table 3.1 (Continued)

1977-81 (Continued)

Miss Winslow & Son, Mork & Mindy, Mrs. Columbo, Mulligan's Stew, Nancy Drew Mysteries, A New Kind of Family, Open All Night, Oregon Trail, Out of the Blue, The Pallisers, Palmerstown USA, Paris, The Ropers, The Runaways, Sanford Arms, Search & Rescue, Secrets of Midland Heights, Shannon, Skag, The Stockard Channing Show, Stone, Tabitha, Thirteen Queens Blvd., Thunder, Too Close for Comfort, Turnabout, The Two of Us, United States, Walking Tall, We've Got Each Other, Who's Watching the Kids, Woobind, Animal Doctor, The Yeagers, The Yellow Rose, The Young Pioneers, Zorro and Son.

1982-86/87

ALF, AKA Pablo, A Year in the Life, Baby Makes Five, Bare Essence, Better Days, Boone, Buck Jones, Butterflies, Cagney & Lacey, Call to Glory, Capitol, Captain Justice, Charles in Charge, Charlie & Company, Condo, The Cosby Show, Crazy Like a Fox, Crime Story, The Devlin Connection, Domestic Life, Double Trouble, The Ellen Burstyn Show, Emerald Point NAS, Everything's Relative, Falcon Crest, Family Ties, Family Tree, Filthy Rich, Foot in the Door, The Four Seasons, Full House, George & Mildred, Gloria, Golden Girls, Growing Pains, Gun Shy, The Hamptons, Heart of the City, Herbie the Love Bug, Hometown, Hot Pursuit, I Married Dora, It Takes Two, It's Not Easy, It's Your Move, Jack & Mike, Jennifer Slept Here, Joani Loves Chachi, Kate & Allie, Kings Crowning, The Law and Harry McGraw, Life with Lucy, Lime Street, Little House: A New Beginning, Loving, Momma Malone, Mama's Family, Matlock, Mr. Belvedere, My Sister Sam, My Two Dads, Newhart, Oh Madeline, Our Honor, Our House, Pac Man, Punky Brewster, Reggie, Reilly, Ace of Spies, The Rousters, Scarecrow & Mrs. King, Seven Brides for Seven Brothers, Sidekicks, Silver Spoons, Simon & Simon, Spencer, Star of the Family, Starman, Thirtysomething, Together We Stand, Tucker's Witch, Two Marriages, 227, Valerie, Webster, A Year in the Life, You Again.

Note: From *Trends in the Portrayal of Families on U.S. Commercial Television,* 1947-1987 by J. P. Murray, 1990, unpublished manuscript, Kansas State University, Department of Human Development and Family Studies, Manhattan.

Educational and
Persuasive Influences
of Television

4

For the most part, the social and emotional messages on television are unintentional and their effects are unplanned. Most entertainment programming is not explicitly designed to teach or influence viewers' actions. Television can, however, be planned so as to teach social values and social behavior as well as academic and cognitive skills. It can be designed to mobilize viewers to take certain actions and it can be used as a forum for airing socially controversial topics.

In this chapter, we consider some types of television that are designed to teach or persuade, sometimes for the benefit of viewers and sometimes for the benefit of product manufacturers. Four topics are included: (1) programs to teach cognitive skills and prosocial behavior, (2) nutrition and health messages, (3) advertising, and (4) programming about controversial social issues. In some cases, unplanned messages are considered in conjunction with the deliberate efforts to educate or persuade.

COGNITIVE SKILLS AND PROSOCIAL BEHAVIOR

Attempts to use television for instruction were begun in the 1950s, but they concentrated on formal instruction, primarily at secondary and college levels. The late 1960s witnessed the beginning of a major effort to use broadcast television for teaching academic skills to young children. This move was stimulated in part by the widespread social concern in the 1960s about poverty and educational disadvantage. In addition, in 1967, the Public Broadcasting Act established a system of noncommercial stations with a mandate to provide diverse cultural and educational programming for both children and adults.

At first, public television was ignored because many people thought it was dull and appealed only to a small audience of highly educated people with esoteric tastes. That stereotype was shattered when a group of educators, psychologists, television writers and producers combined their talents to create *Sesame Street* and *The Electric Company*. Production techniques from advertising and cartoons were used to package information about reading, cognitive skills, self-esteem, and prosocial behavior. *Sesame Street* was successful beyond anyone's expectations in reaching an audience of preschoolers, including many who were poor and educationally disadvantaged. Since that time, other educational programs designed to teach science (*3-2-1 Contact*) and math (*Square One*) have been created. *Reading Rainbow* has been remarkably successful in achieving its goal of stimulating children's interest in books. These programs reach a large number of children from a wide range of social groups.

Evaluations have demonstrated that children learn letters, numbers, and other cognitive skills from these programs. *Sesame Street* was evaluated in several parts of the country during its first two years. In the first year, children who watched the program frequently were compared with those who did not. In the second, the researchers used a field experimental design in which children were randomly assigned to view or not to view the program at home. The experimental group was given cable connections or UHF sets (necessary to receive the program), and their mothers were asked to encourage the children to watch the program. The control group did not receive extra television reception aids or encouragement to view. Both groups of children took a test of cognitive skills before and after the viewing season (about 6 months). The results of the two evaluations were consistent with each other. The children who watched *Sesame Street* regularly learned more than those who did not. Gains in the measured skills occurred for girls and boys from a variety of social backgrounds (Ball & Bogatz, 1970; Bogatz & Ball, 1971; Cook et al., 1975).

A more recent longitudinal study demonstrated that children's vocabularies improved when they watched *Sesame Street* regularly between the ages of 3 and 5 (Rice, Huston, Truglio, & Wright, 1990).

Similar evaluations were conducted for *The Electric Company*. Children who saw the program in school benefited from viewing it, but home viewing alone did not increase reading skills of children who were attending school. No information about individuals not in school (either young children or older drop-outs) was obtained (Ball & Bogatz, 1973).

The potential educational effects of television have been doubted, in part because the broadcast medium does not allow the "teacher" to be responsive to individual viewers' needs. The pace is invariant, viewers cannot ask questions or ask for repetition, the scheduling is inflexible, and it is difficult to build on earlier lessons. With the advent of inexpensive, portable videotape recorders, many of these limitations no longer exist. A wide range of programming for in-school use is creative, lively, and varied. Schools pay for permission to videotape educational programming and are then free to use the videotapes in whatever contexts and time periods they like.

Planned programming can also teach prosocial behavior and values (Fairchild, 1984; Gunter, 1981; Rushton, 1979, 1982). One of the longest running programs for preschool children is *Mister Rogers' Neighborhood*. Several investigations have demonstrated that children learn such positive behaviors as nurturance and sympathy, task persistence, empathy, and imaginativeness from viewing the program (Coates, Pusser, & Goodman, 1976; Singer & Singer, 1981; Stein & Friedrich, 1975; Tower, Singer, Singer, & Biggs, 1979). Some of these investigations were field experiments in which one group of children was assigned to view the program, and a control group watched another program. Children in the experimental treatments demonstrated prosocial behaviors in natural settings when playing with other children and adults (Friedrich & Stein, 1973; Stein & Friedrich, 1972). In a subsequent study of economically disadvantaged children, the effects of the program were enhanced by providing relevant play materials to be used in verbal rehearsal and role-playing of program themes after viewing (Friedrich & Stein, 1975; Friedrich-Cofer, Huston-Stein, Kipnis, Susman, & Clewett, 1979).

Several other programs designed to teach prosocial behavior were produced in the 1970s. One notable success on commercial television was *Fat Albert and the Cosby Kids*. Issues of importance in children's lives, such as divorce, friendship, child abuse, and drugs, were presented. Numerous investigations demonstrated that children understood the messages of the program and were able to apply them (CBS Broadcast Group, 1974; Calvert, Huston, Watkins, & Wright, 1982; Calvert, Huston, & Wright, 1987).

NUTRITION AND HEALTH

Television is a major source of information about physical health. Programs frequently deal with health issues, and health remedies are often advertised. The medium also has real promise for planned messages about physical and mental health. For the most part, planned messages occur in advertisements and public service announcements rather than in the programs they surround, but, of course, the content of the programs is important as well.

Illness and Treatment of Health Problems

Doctors, nurses, hospitals, and illness are portrayed frequently on television, but in many respects television presents a distorted picture of illness and medical treatment. In an analysis of commercials and programs on prime-time television over two weeks, acute illness and injury were often portrayed; chronic illness and the long-term consequences of illness were shown less often. Doctors rarely made diagnostic errors, and health professionals other than doctors and nurses were rarely shown. Biomedical treatments (including drugs) and hospital care were emphasized instead of interpersonal or home-based ways of dealing with illness. Some current issues in the health field (e.g., cost containment, lack of availability) were not dealt with. Advertisements also emphasized over-the-counter drugs as a remedy for aches, pains, and ills of all kinds (Turow & Coe, 1985).

Children who are heavy viewers of television show high concern about getting sick and have heightened perceptions of the relief they can get from medicines. They have relatively positive attitudes about legal drugs (over-the-counter remedies), but there is no evidence at present that such positive attitudes extend to illegal drugs (Atkin, 1978). There is little evidence about adult perceptions or behavior in this domain.

Health Campaigns

Media campaigns to promote health have been used and evaluated in a variety of studies (cf. Solomon, 1982). Media campaigns to promote healthy practices can be successful, but there is some disagreement about what factors are associated with success. One author (Wallack, 1983) suggests that health-education campaigns will not succeed on commercial television so long as poor health practices (e.g., alcohol abuse) appear in the programs and advertisements that are supported by those with vested financial interests. Another review (Simpkins & Brenner, 1984) suggests that the contradictory findings stem from individual differences among viewers; viewer perceptions must be taken into account.

Television appears to be an especially potent medium for conveying information about health and nutrition, especially for reaching poorly educated people. Ettema, Brown, and Luepker (1983) found that an information campaign about cardiovascular health increased viewers' knowledge and decreased the knowledge gap between individuals of higher and lower socioeconomic status. Television was more effective than other media in a national campaign in Australia about disabled persons. It was most effective for creating awareness, but less effective for changing attitudes and behavior (Gething, 1984).

The Hyatt-Regency disaster in Kansas City occurred when a walkway collapsed, killing and injuring a large number of people at a dance in the lobby below it. Psychologists developed and disseminated media materials related to disaster reactions and mental health to the Kansas City community. Gist and Stolz (1982) describe a process for distributing such materials to reduce community mental-health problems.

Changing technology has opened the way for the use of video materials to promote health. Videotapes are used for in-service training of health professionals and staff development (e.g., Van Son, 1982). In hospitals and physicians' offices, people who are waiting are offered the opportunity to watch videotapes on health practices such as self-examination for breast lumps or rehabilitative exercises. Such informative uses of television appear to have considerable potential, and they overcome some of the problems inherent in broadcast television of targeting particular groups within a mass audience.

Nutrition

Both television viewing as an activity and messages about food in television content, are alleged to play roles in establishing lasting patterns of food preference, eating behavior, and physical activity levels in leisure time. Television programs and advertisements portray food consumption and contain frequent inducements to eat and drink that could affect consumption while viewing as well as eating habits in other situations.

Programs portray eating and drinking practices that are probably not conducive to good health. Prime-time programs contain frequent references to food—more frequent than those in commercials (Kaufman, 1980). Characters often eat snacks rather than organized meals, a practice known as "grazing" (Gerbner et al., 1982). The imbalance is even greater in weekend children's programs (Gerbner et al., 1982). People on television drink a lot of alcohol and coffee (Kaufman, 1980), but smoking is relatively rare (Gerbner et al., 1982). Despite their patterns of eating, television characters are rarely overweight; only 12% of adults shown are obese, and 90% of the obese persons are black (Palumbo & Dietz, 1985). One analyst summarized her findings as follows: "The television 'diet' may be unbalanced and fattening, but characters in commercials and programs alike remain slim and healthy" (Kaufman, 1980, p.37).

Dental problems and obesity are health consequences that could result from following the nutritional practices shown on television. Dietz and Gortmaker (1985) documented a clear association between television viewing and obesity among children and adolescents in a nationally representative health survey of over 15,000 subjects. The probability of obesity increased by 2% with every hour per day of television viewed, even when a variety of family and environmental variables were statistically controlled. One sample of 2,153 subjects was studied on two occasions separated by three or four years; the subjects' television viewing predicted increases in obesity on the second occasion, even with initial obesity statistically controlled. The amount of obesity was not related to time spent reading or with friends. The authors concluded that television viewing causes obesity. A smaller survey of adolescent males did not show a correlation of television viewing with obesity, but did demonstrate a relationship between physical fitness and television viewing. The more television viewed, the less fit the subjects were (Tucker, 1986). Correlational evidence also suggests a relationship between television viewing by adults and their complacency about nutrition and smoking, but not about alcohol consumption (Gerbner et al., 1982).

Television can also promote positive eating practices. Public service announcements for nutrition and healthy food consumption appear to have some positive effects on children. Nutritional messages in a children's program (*Fat Albert*) had positive effects on children's food choices, particularly when not accompanied by advertisements for junk food (Goldberg, Gorn, & Gibson, 1978).

Future research could be usefully directed to disentangling three possible contributors to the association between television viewing and obesity: (a) television viewing is a low energy activity, (b) people tend to eat snacks while they watch television, and (c) the content of programs and advertisements promote the consumption of calorie-dense foods, with the implication that people who consume these foods rarely get fat. Advertising in particular is designed to induce consumption of food, as well as the use of many other products. We turn now to a discussion of advertising, its effects on nutrition and on other forms of behavior.

ADVERTISING

Advertising embodies commercial television's explicit efforts to use the medium for persuasion. Although advertising is sometimes

considered annoying to adults, most social commentators have
not expressed serious concerns about harmful effects on adults,
except possibly when advertisements are deceitful. Research on
such advertising was recently reviewed by Alwitt & Mitchell
(1985).

Advertising to children, on the other hand, has generated a
good deal of social concern (e.g., Federal Trade Commission,
1978). Commercials directed to child audiences occur primarily
on Saturday and Sunday mornings and on weekdays between 3:00
and 6:00 p.m. on programs for which the majority of the viewing
audience is children. The amount of time devoted to advertising
has fluctuated between about 15% and 20% of each broadcast
hour, depending on the political climate and the amount of federal
regulation or threat of regulation. Given variations in the amount
of television viewing by people of different ages, these figures
suggest an annual exposure to about 20,000 commercial messages
for the average child (Adler & Faber, 1980). After federal deregulation in 1984, the time devoted to advertising and the number
of messages increased (see Figure 4.1) (Condry, Bence, & Schiebe,
1988; Kunkel, 1987).

Content

The products advertised on programs directed to children consist
primarily of food. Analyses in the 1970s showed that the majority
of products advertised were cereals, candy, calorie-dense snack
foods, and food from fast-food restaurants. Over half of these
products were heavily sugared foods, and many others had high
fat content. There were few advertisements for milk products or
other foods (Atkin & Heald, 1977; Barcus, 1977). A similar analysis in 1984 (Condry et al., 1988) showed some reduction in total
advertising, but food products still constituted about 60% of the
commercials on Saturday-morning television; they appeared at a
rate of about 8 per hour. On television designed for general audiences, approximately 25% of the commercials are for foods.
The majority of foods advertised are prepared foods, sweets,
snacks, or products high in fats, cholesterol, sugar, and salt (Gerbner et al., 1982; Kaufman, 1980).

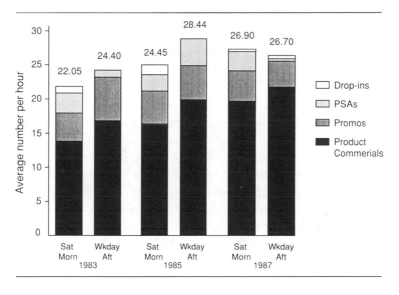

Figure 4.1. Frequency of nonprogram messages on Saturday morning and weekday afternoons, by message type and year. From "The Non-program Content of Children's Television" by J. Condry, P. Bence, and C. Scheibe, 1988, *Journal of Broadcasting and Electronic Media, 32,* 255–270, Figure 4. Reprinted by permission of the Broadcast Education Association.

Toys are the other major products advertised to children. The proportion of advertisements devoted to toys varies seasonally, with heavy emphasis during the fall pre-Christmas months (Barcus, 1980). In the 1980s, a new form of product-related programming appeared—what Peggy Charren of Action for Children's Television called the 30-minute commercial. Most of the new programs introduced on commercial television were designed to feature merchandised toys (e.g., *The Transformers, Ghostbusters*).

Commercials aimed at children rely on a limited number of presentational techniques. Most often an on-camera person or character presents information (Winick, Williamson, Chuzmir, & Winick, 1973). The vast majority of commercials are at least partly animated and use fantasy settings and characters (Barcus, 1980; Doolittle & Pepper, 1975). Excitement is often associated with products by presenting them in action or in aggression-oriented contexts (Schuetz & Sprafkin, 1979; Winick et al., 1973). Boys appear more often than girls in most types of advertisements (Doolittle & Pepper, 1975; Feldstein & Feldstein, 1982; Macklin & Kolbe, 1984; Schuetz & Sprafkin, 1979).

Some part of the commercial message is typically repeated about four times, both visually and verbally, and most messages involve some sort of qualifier or disclaimer, such as "some assembly required" or "it may not improve your child's grades, but it will make learning more fun" (Barcus, 1980). However, such qualifiers or disclaimers are often not understood by children (Liebert, Sprafkin, Liebert, & Rubinstein, 1977).

Objective information about the product is usually scarce in advertisements. Instead, commercials rely on verbal assertions about the subjective qualities of the product (e.g., "it's delicious"), and descriptions of the physical components of the product ("8% by weight"). Advertisements to children stress such food qualities as taste, texture, appearance, fun associations, and accompanying prizes as reasons for choosing foods. Nutritional information is usually brief or nonexistent. Products are sometimes lauded for making the consumer strong, but "being good for you" is rarely stressed. In fact, advertisements often imply that a healthy food is unpalatable by saying it tastes great despite the fact that it is healthy (Barcus, 1977).

Cognitive Abilities Necessary to Process Advertising
In order to respond to commercials in an adult manner, a child must be able to (a) discriminate the commercial from the rest of the programming, and (b) understand the persuasive intent of the commercial content. Young children (under about 7 or 8 years old) are able to distinguish commercial from noncommercial content if the assessment method is primarily nonverbal (e.g., looking at a bit of television and saying whether it is a commercial or a program) (Ward, Levinson, & Wackman, 1972; Ward, Reale & Wackman, 1972). Children age 4 and below often cannot make even a nonverbal distinction (Butter, Popovitch, Stackhouse, & Garner, 1981; Donohue, Henke, & Donohue, 1980; Levin, Petros, & Petrella, 1982; Stephens & Stutts, 1982). Children over

age 7 or 8 can describe the features of commercials that make them different from programs (Blatt, Spencer, & Ward, 1972; Robertson & Rossiter, 1974; Ward, Reale, & Levinson, 1972; Ward, Wackman, & Wartella, 1977). Both age and the form of questioning are related to children's understanding of the persuasive intent of commercials. Children under about 7 or 8 years old have difficulty describing the purposes of commercials, though they may recognize the correct answers in a multiple choice format (Donohue, Meyer, & Henke, 1978; Paget, Kritt, & Bergemann, 1984; Reid, 1979; Robertson & Rossiter, 1974; Rossiter & Robertson, 1974; Ward et al., 1977). Of course, awareness of commercial intent by itself is not sufficient to prevent susceptibility to advertising, even for adolescents (Linn, de Benedectis, & Delucchi, 1982; Ross et al., 1984).

Audiovisual inserts designed to mark the changes from program to commercials were adopted by children's broadcasters in the 1970s in response to federal regulation efforts. Although these separators were intended to aid children, they are ineffective in helping children to discriminate programs from commercials except in cases where they contain simple and explicit labeling (e.g., "Now, we'll have a commercial") (Ballard-Campbell, 1983; Palmer & McDowell, 1979; Stutts, Vance, & Hudleson, 1981).

Responses to Television Advertising

The appeal of commercials declines as children mature. Children younger than about 7 attend to commercials as much as to regular program content, but older children get less attentive when the advertisements come on. Coupled with this decline is an increase in skepticism or distrust in the truthfulness of commercials (Bearden, Teel, & Wright, 1979; Moore & Stephens, 1975; Robertson & Rossiter, 1974; Rossiter, 1977; Ward, 1972; Ward et al., 1977).

Studies of children's responses to commercials provide fairly strong evidence that children's information, knowledge, and preferences are affected (see Adler et al., 1980; Atkin, 1982; Federal Trade Commission, 1978; Roedder, Sternhal, & Calder, 1983; Stoneman & Brody, 1983). Total television viewing is correlated with the eating patterns that one might expect television to encourage. For example, heavy television viewers reported eating larger amounts of sugar, cereal, candy, potato chips, hot dogs, and soda pop than light viewers. Heavy viewers also have relatively low levels of nutritional knowledge and are less accurate in evaluating nutrition claims in food commercials.

Heavy viewers of advertising request advertised products more often than light viewers (Atkin, 1982). In one investigation, children were observed in the grocery store with their mothers. Requests for frequently advertised foods correlated with the amount of commercial television the children watched at home, but not with the amount of public television viewed (Galst & White, 1976). Requests for products become more frequent with increasing age until about age 8, then they decline (Atkin, 1975a; Caron & Ward, 1975; Clancy-Hepburn, Hickey, & Neville, 1974; Robertson & Rossiter, 1976, 1977; Robertson, Rossiter, & Gleason, 1979; Ward & Wackman, 1972; Wells, 1965). Heavy viewers also express greater desire for advertised products in surveys and experiments, even if the product is intended for adults (Goldberg & Gorn, 1974; Goldberg & Gorn, 1978; Gorn & Florsheim, 1985; Gorn & Goldberg, 1977; Resnik & Stern, 1977; Sheikh & Moleski, 1977). Heavy viewing does not immunize children against commercial appeals nor does it help them to be more sophisticated about the persuasive intent of commercials. There is no evidence to support the notion that exposure to commercials serves as a form of consumer socialization.

Exposure to commercials probably affects consumption, but experimental studies of advertising effects have produced mixed findings on this issue. Some experimental studies of preschoolers have shown effects of advertisements on children's snack choices after brief exposures during a television program (Lemnitzer, Jeffrey, Hess, Hickey, & Stroud, 1979); others have found little effect (Jerome, 1982). Some experimental studies have shown effects on children's stated food preferences. Goldberg, Gorn, and Gibson (1978) found that children's choices were influenced by advertisements for highly sugared foods or for fruits and vegetables. Moreover, a children's program devoted to pronutrition messages was highly effective in influencing children to choose nonsugared snacks. When advertising does influence consumption, the effects occur for a whole class of products (e.g., candy bars), not just for the brand advertised (Atkin, 1982).

Product appeal is greater for black children if there is a black character in the commercial, but a character's ethnicity does not appear to matter much to white children (Barry & Hansen, 1973). Celebrity endorsers and premiums enhance the appeal of advertised products (Atkin & Block, 1983; Kunkel, 1988a; Ross et al., 1984).

Commercials may lead to family conflict when parents refuse to purchase advertised products (Atkin, 1975b). About half of the children in one survey reported arguing with mothers at least sometimes after being denied a requested toy, and about the same proportion reported becoming angry at least sometimes after such a denial. Children sometimes feel sad or angry as a result of television commercials; for instance, heavy viewers expressed disappointment over not receiving Christmas gifts they wanted (Robertson & Rossiter, 1976). Some children report feeling bad when seeing commercials depicting people better off than they are (Atkin, 1975b; Donohue et al., 1978). Many report feeling irritated that the program they were viewing was interrupted (Atkin, 1975b).

Conclusions

With federal deregulation in the early 1980s, the amounts and types of advertising to children increased. Some regular form of content analysis is needed to monitor trends in advertising so that policymakers can make informed decisions. There are many questions about advertising effects that have barely been addressed. For instance, does heavy viewing of commercials make children more materialistic as they get older? Does the regular interruption of programming for commercial messages lead to a decrease in the ability to maintain attention in other situations? What are the long-term effects of exposure to commercials, especially health-related commercials, on attitudes toward health and on the actual health of viewers? Are there individual differences in persuasability, in addition to or in interaction with other individual differences (age, sex, ethnicity) that ought to be investigated vis-à-vis exposure to commercials? With issues like these remaining to be addressed, it would seem advisable to rekindle research interest in children and television advertising.

SOCIAL ISSUES

In the last several years, there have been many news programs, talk shows, documentaries, docudramas, and television movies dealing with such social issues as homelessness, teenage pregnancy, child abuse, and the AIDS crisis. These programs often are praised as efforts to use television to provide insight into serious social problems rather than as light entertainment. Even when issues are presented in dramatic form, the producers often intend their efforts to air socially controversial issues.

Does such programming serve an educational purpose? Does it increase viewers' knowledge and awareness of the problems in their society? Does it stimulate thoughtful consideration of the issues? If these were the only questions, there would probably be little debate. However, many observers have worried that such presentations may stimulate the socially maladaptive behavior they seek to expose and explore. Does a program about an abused wife who burns her husband in his bed instigate such violence in even a few of the millions of viewers who see it? Does a program about an adolescent suicide tip the balance toward suicide for even a few young people? Of course, this question is especially pressing when suicide is the potential consequence.

Specific programs do have at least a short term impact. For example, a 1985 *60 Minutes* program on a black slum in Tunica, Mississippi, resulted in the town being innundated with gifts of used clothing and food, a dozen families were moved from their shacks into mobile homes, and rent-subsidized housing was also built (Moss, 1987). Similarly, the massive increase in contributions to Ethiopia in 1984 after a major news story on the famine there is a well-documented example of the power of the medium to influence attitudes and behaviors.

The coverage of these issues may be too erratic to have any long-term or more generalized impact, but little empirical evidence is available. However, surveys show that viewers believe that television can help prevent social problems; for example, 69% of adults in one survey believed that condom commercials should be shown on television in order to prevent sexually transmitted diseases (American Institute for Public Opinion Research, March 23, 1987).

Several studies assessed the impact of a widely advertised program on nuclear war entitled *The Day After* (Feldman & Sigelman, 1985; Oskamp et al., 1985). Attitudes were measured before and after the program was televised; however, an enormous amount of coverage in other media preceded this program, discussing both the issue and the specific program. For that reason, the impact of the program may have been influenced by other media coverage.

In contrast to the dearth of research on television coverage of most social issues, there is a growing body of literature on television's impact on suicide. One researcher, David P. Phillips, a sociologist at the University of California at San Diego, has conducted most of the research on this topic. In the 1970s, Phillips and his colleagues published several articles describing increases in suicides, motor-vehicle accidents, and noncommercial airline crashes following newspaper stories on suicides (see Phillips, 1986, for a review of this literature).

In the 1980s, Phillips and his colleagues turned their attention to television news coverage (Phillips, 1983). Bollen and Phillips (1982) examined United States daily mortality data collected by the National Center for Health Statistics (NCHS) between 1972 and 1976. They listed all television news stories of individual suicides and analyzed those stories that appeared on at least two network evening news programs. They compared suicide rates for the week before and the week after the suicide story and found a 7% increase. There were two peaks, one on the day of and the day after the story aired, and the other on the 6th and 7th days after. They concluded that the impact of the suicide story lasts approximately 10 days, and that this impact was significant when other variables that are known to influence suicide rates are statistically controlled, such as the day of the week, the month, and holidays.

Phillips (1982) also studied fictional suicides on television and reported similar results. For example, suicide attempts on television soap operas were related to an increase in suicides and motor-vehicle fatalities during the week of the suicide story, compared to the week before. The increase in car crashes was due to single-vehicle crashes, which Phillips speculated were disguised suicides. He also found an increase in nonfatal single-vehicle crashes in California, which was the only state that had such data.

Kessler and Stipp (1984) replicated Phillips' soap opera study, with dramatically different results. They claimed that Phillips sometimes made important errors in calculating the dates that the soap opera suicides were broadcast and that one of his comparison weeks that accounted for most of the significant difference was inappropriately selected. Kessler and Stipp studied the actual day of the soap-opera suicide and the next three days, and found no increase in suicides or car accidents.

Horton and Stack (1984) examined the relationship between the amount of time spent on suicide stories for all network evening news programs and the monthly suicide rates between 1972 and 1980. They controlled for unemployment rates, divorce rates, and time of year and found no effect of the suicide stories. This suggests that the number of seconds spent on a news story may not be the important variable or that the impact of suicide stories is only significant in the short term, perhaps over the 10-day period that Phillips described.

Most recently, the impact on teenagers of television coverage of suicides has been the focus of research. Phillips and Carstensen (1986) reported that teenage suicides increased following nationally televised news or feature stories, and that this increase was greater than for adult suicides. They found no difference between the impact of general-information or feature stories about suicide and news stories about a particular suicide. This study was based on 38 stories broadcast between 1973 and 1979.

Gould and Shaffer (1986) found an increased number of suicides and attempted suicides in the greater New York area during the two weeks after four fictional television films were broadcast in 1984 and 1985. However, Phillips and Paight (1987) replicated this study and found that the same programs had no impact on suicides in California and Pennsylvania. In fact, the trends, although nonsignificant, were in the opposite direction. They concluded that neither the urban nor northeastern characteristics of the Gould and Shaffer sample could explain the difference in results, but they did not speculate on why the results of their study of California and Pennsylvania teenagers were so different from Phillips' previous research on adult suicides.

All of the films studied by Gould and Shaffer (1986) were accompanied by educational and preventive materials that were made available to local network affiliates for distribution. There was no increase in completed suicides related to the one program that included even greater efforts at prevention: the distribution of teachers' guides to classrooms around the country and the display of phone numbers of suicide prevention hot lines during and after the film.

Overall, the studies on television suicides show how the impact of television on social issues may be dramatically different from the intended result. These studies also show some of the difficulties inherent in assessing the impact of television on social issues; there are large numbers of viewers and such outcomes as suicide are infrequent. Hence, such studies are complicated and difficult to conduct and to replicate.

SUMMARY AND CONCLUSIONS

Broadcast television can be used effectively for teaching cognitive skills and prosocial behavior. Programs for a variety of different ages teach academic skills and knowledge and convey cooperative and helpful ways of dealing with others, understanding of such problems as child abuse and divorce, and the excitement of learning. Planned programs for children were developed in the 1960s partly because public television provided a noncommercial outlet. They continued to be developed in the 1970s as public funds were available, but declined in the 1980s as public concern about children and the disadvantaged seemed to decline and government support for public broadcasting was reduced. There is a large body of evidence showing that planned programming is effective in teaching academic skills and prosocial behavior.

Television carries a wide range of messages about health and nutrition. Entertainment programming is crowded with medical settings in which crisis situations prevail and biomedical treatments predominate. Programming that is specifically designed to convey health messages (e.g., diet and exercise for a healthy heart) can increase people's knowledge, but there is little evidence about its effects on behavior. Television programs and advertisements promote foods that are apt to contribute to obesity and dental problems, and there is some evidence that frequent television viewing contributes to obesity.

Children are exposed to at least an hour of television commercials for every five hours of commercial programming they view. There can be little doubt that young children (below about age 7) have difficulty distinguishing commercials from programs and evaluating the persuasive intent of advertisements. Moreover, viewing commercials increases the product's appeal and the child's desire for and consumption of advertised products. Exposure does not lead children to become sophisticated consumers by virtue of mere experience with advertising. In fact, heavy viewers are more likely than light viewers to believe commercial claims. A child's desire for expensive products can lead to parent-child conflict and disappointment with the types of toys and foods the parent provides.

The extent to which one ought to be concerned about these issues is dictated in part by the kinds of products advertised. At present, they consist primarily of calorie-dense foods with high concentrations of fats and sugar. Toys of varying quality represent most of the remaining products. In recent years, product-related programs have served as another means for promoting toys—a trend that has caused some critics to argue that much of children's television is now 100% advertising.

Television presentations of such dramatic social issues as suicides or spouse abuse may have paradoxical effects. They may raise awareness of social problems and even provide opportunities for affected individuals to seek help. However, in the case of suicides, they may also instigate suicide attempts by susceptible individuals. We need to know more about what elements in the presentation of these issues influence viewers' responses and what preventive measures are effective.

5

When people talk about television, they usually describe its content. Content analyses tell us how much violence, prosocial behavior, stereotyping, or emotional expression is in a sample of programs. Viewers select programs with content they enjoy or that suits their needs for information or entertainment. But what is distinctive about television is its form, not its content. Its combination of visual and auditory images is compelling and seemingly natural. Unlike the codes of print media, people can understand television's basic codes without extensive learning. Of course, the sophisticated analyst is aware that the images created are not simple replications of the real world—they are the result of planning, selection, and organizing at several levels of filming and editing. The temporal order of events can be arbitrary. Many conventions are particular to the medium, and a viewer who does not know the conventions may well be confused. For example, instant replays are so widely used in sports that they are often not marked with narration or visual clues; viewers who do not know that may find themselves wondering why the action changes and repeats in such bizarre ways.

Since the early days of television, some theorists and critics have contended that the medium itself affects its audience, regardless of its content. One theme of these commentaries is the displacement hypothesis—the notion that television influences both learning and social behavior by displacing such activities as reading, family interaction, and social play with peers. This hypothesis is intuitively reasonable in light of the large amount of time that people spend watching television. Surely some other activities must be curtailed.

A second theme is the notion that television as a medium affects the structure of thought or the nature of cognitive processing. McLuhan (1964) proposed that television cultivates forms of thought that are fundamentally different from those used in processing print or some other media. Salomon (1979) argued that audiences not only learn to interpret filmic codes, but incorporate some of those codes as modes of processing nontelevision information. Huston and Wright (1989) proposed that the form and structure of the medium influence both attention to and comprehension of the messages conveyed. Singer (1980) argued that the rapid pace and sensory complexity of most television lead to shallow processing and behavioral disorganization in young children.

A third theme is passivity. Because television is typically a spectator medium, many critics have argued that it encourages passive intellectual processing and a passive approach to life. Entertainment is served up in predigested packages; the consumer does not need to organize, initiate, or invent. These critics are especially concerned that large doses of television will reduce imagination and creativity (Lesser, 1977; Winn, 1987).

METHODS OF STUDY

The effects of television as a medium are difficult to evaluate because virtually everyone is exposed to it. The existing small groups of nonviewers cannot be studied for comparison to viewers, because they probably differ from television users in many characteristics other than their exposure to television. During the 1950s, several investigators (Belson, 1967; Himmelweit, Oppenheim, & Vince, 1958; Schramm, Lyle, & Parker, 1961) studied the introduction of television into society, but, because the medium spread so quickly, only one of these studies (Schramm et al., 1961) included an evaluation of comparable locales with and without television. In the early 1970s, investigators in British Columbia and Australia studied natural experiments, that is, conditions existing naturally that allowed them to make comparative studies (which will be discussed in more detail later). They located towns that did not have television reception and towns that were similar in other respects that did receive television (Murray, 1980; Murray & Kippax, 1978; Williams, 1986). In both Australia and British Columbia, the researchers returned two years later after television was introduced into the no-television town.

The majority of investigations rely on correlations between the amount of television viewed and the outcome variables of interest. When such investigations are longitudinal or contain very large samples, they can employ statistical controls for the many confounding factors associated with the amount of viewing (e.g., education, social class, race, gender, intelligence) so that they provide persuasive evidence for causal relationships.

At a more microscopic level, cross-media comparisons have been used. Comparable content is presented by television, radio, and print, and outcomes are measured in a laboratory situation. Variations in television format, structure, or formal features are used similarly in experimental investigations of attention, comprehension, and social behavior.

In this chapter we examine the effects of the television medium on social behavior and leisure time, academic and intellectual performance, and cognitive processing. Individual differences are then considered, followed by a consideration of passivity, involvement, and effort. Finally, the effects of the forms and formats on television are discussed.

SOCIAL BEHAVIOR AND LEISURE TIME

Television affects the structuring of leisure time partly through displacement. Both children and adults reduced their use of radio, records, movies, and similar media when television was introduced in their communities, but the effects on print-media use were less clear. The early investigators of television concluded from these findings that the activities most often displaced were functionally equivalent to television—listening to the radio, attending movies, and reading comic books (Schramm et al., 1961). Television also leads to reduced participation in community activities, especially sports, clubs, dances, and parties (Murray & Kippax, 1978; Williams, 1986). After television is introduced, adults spend more time in such home hobbies as needlepoint and carpentry, perhaps because they can be combined with television viewing (Murray & Kippax, 1978).

The impact of television on leisure-time activities for both children and adults is demonstrated in the comparisons of three towns in Australia: a no-television town, a low-television town, which had been receiving television for one year, and a high-television town, which had received television for five years (Murray & Kippax, 1978). Four clusters of leisure time activities were examined: (1) alternative media (radio, reading material, records, cinema, theater and concerts, and public talks), (2) social engagement (social visits, dances and clubs, indoor activities, group activities, outdoor activities, playing sports, and spectator sports), (3) individual interests (hobbies and animal care), and (4) time filling (driving around and sitting around doing nothing). The times spent in each category are shown in Figure 5.1. Comparisons between the no-television town and the low-television town show marked decrements in all categories for children and in three of the four for adults.

Some of the displacement effects, however, appear to be a response to the novelty of television. They wear off after the medium has been available for a while. Most clusters of activity were higher in the high-television town than in the low-television town, and when television was introduced into the no-television town, leisure-time activities away from home declined below such activities in the other two towns (Figure 5.2).

Television has less clear effects on social interaction within families and with peers outside the family than on leisure-time activities. When television was introduced, families did not spend less time together, but some people argue that time watching television together is lower in quality than other types of interaction. Heavy television viewers spend slightly less time with peers than light viewers, but the causal direction involved is not clear (Dorr, 1986). Moreover, when children watch television together,

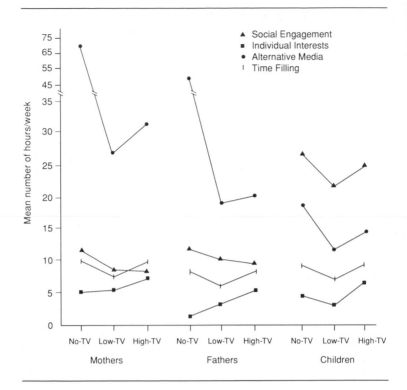

Figure 5.1. Parents' and children's activity patterns in three towns with differing television experience. From *Television and Youth: 25 Years of Research and Controversy* by J. P. Murray, 1980, Boys Town, NE: Boys Town Center for the Study of Youth Development. Reprinted by permission of author.

their play is less active—that is, they are less talkative, less physically active, and less aggressive than during play without television (Gadberry, 1974).

These findings support a modified version of the displacement hypothesis. Television viewing does displace other activities, but not at random. They are activities that serve functions similar to television (e.g., entertainment) and those that are incompatible with viewing (e.g., attending a local sports event). Moreover, the impact of television on other activities is not static; the role of television in people's lives changes over time. When it is introduced, there are novelty effects that wear off. It gradually becomes a background rather than a foreground for many activities, and at the same time, it becomes a pervasive part of everyday life. Most people under the age of 40 have difficulty imagining a world without television.

ACADEMIC AND INTELLECTUAL PERFORMANCE

Large-scale correlational studies consistently show a small relation between heavy television viewing and poor school achievement. In a meta-analysis of 23 studies involving thousands of children, the curvilinear pattern shown in Figure 5.3 emerged. Achievement improved with increased television viewing up to about 10 hours a week. For children who watched more than 10 hours a week, achievement declined as viewing time increased (Williams, Haertel, Walberg, & Haertel, 1982).

Although children from lower social-class homes watch more television and perform less well in school than those from middle-class homes, the association between viewing and achievement holds true even within social classes. However, intelligence does appear to account for much of the negative relation between viewing and school achievement. For children of equivalent intelligence, there is little or no association between television viewing and most types of school achievement or cognitive functioning (Anderson & Collins, 1988).

Reading is the one subject that may be negatively influenced by television viewing, but the effects are small. In the British Columbia study, for example, early elementary children in the town without television performed better on reading tests than the children whose towns received television. Two years later, after television was introduced in the no-television town, children in the early grades had poorer reading skills than their counterparts of two years earlier (Corteen & Williams, 1986).

Among children in the United States who have grown up with television, heavy viewing of entertainment television is slightly associated with poor reading skills (Morgan & Gross, 1982; Truglio, Huston, & Wright, 1986). However, reading skill is much

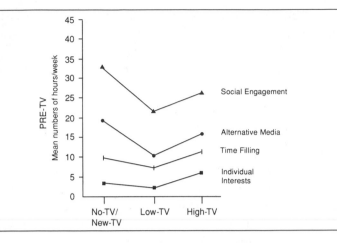

Figure 5.2. Children's activity patterns before and after the introduction of television. From *Television and Youth: 25 Years of Research and Controversy* by J. P.

more directly affected by practice and attitudes about print. Children who watch television and become involved with books are apt to become good readers (Morgan & Gross, 1982; Ritchie, Price, & Roberts, 1987).

Different types of television programs have different effects on achievement and cognitive functioning. We have already pointed out that children learn vocabulary, letters, and number skills from such programs as *Sesame Street* and *The Electric Company* (Chapter 4). Documentaries and instructional television can be used effectively to teach a wide range of information (Liebert & Sprafkin, 1988).

In summary, television as a medium does not have any clear effect on children's school achievement or on academic skill. Children who spend a great deal of time viewing television do poorly in school, but the reasons seem to lie in individual differences in intelligence, motivation, or family environments. Children who watch a moderate amount of television perform better in school than nonviewers, perhaps because they seek a variety of sources of information and entertainment or because they use the medium at its best rather than its worst.

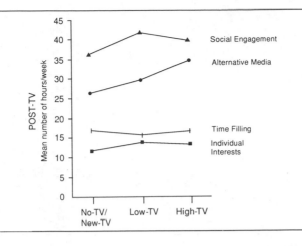

Murray, 1980, Boys Town, NE: Boys Town Center for the Study of Youth Development. Reprinted by permission of author.

COGNITIVE PROCESSING AND TELEVISION

McLuhan's basic notion that "the medium is the message" has had a wide appeal to scholars as well as others, but translating it into a more specific theory or verifiable hypotheses has proved to be a formidable task. Salomon (1979) conducted a series of investigations that demonstrated that children could learn specific mental skills from seeing certain filmic codes. For instance, watching slow zooms in to details of a large picture taught children visual analytic skills. A group of Israeli children who watched *Sesame Street* showed improved ability to take different spatial perspectives when looking at a setting. Greenfield (1984) also cited some evidence to support the hypothesis that television may promote visual spatial skills and be particularly well-suited for conveying information using motion, animation, and close-up photography. On the whole, however, the evidence for lasting changes in cognitive processing as a result of television viewing is weak (Anderson & Collins, 1988).

The hypothesis that television leads to a loss of creativity and imagination has met a similar fate; it is difficult to test and the existing evidence provides little support. In the British Columbia

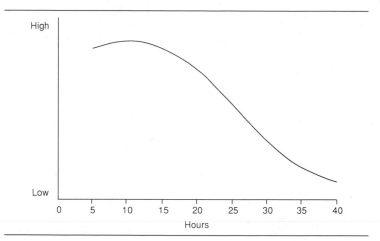

Figure 5.3. Estimated relationship of achievement to weekly hours of television viewing, based on a meta-analysis. From "The Impact of Leisure-Time Television on School Learning: A Research Synthesis" by P. A. Williams, E. H. Haertel, H. J. Walberg, and G. D. Haertel, 1982, *American Educational Research Journal, 19*, 19–50, Figure 2. Copyright 1982 by the American Educational Research Association. Reprinted by permission of the publisher.

study, children showed reduced performance on one of two measures of creativity after television was introduced (Harrison & Williams, 1986). Cross-media investigations comparing radio with television show that children generate visual images when listening, but television inspires different types of imaginative activities. It is arbitrary to decide that one type of imagining is of a higher quality than the other (Anderson & Collins, 1988). Moreover, any casual observer of children is well aware that television characters and content serve as the basis for a great deal of imaginative play.

Still another popular criticism of television is the notion that rapidly paced television reduces children's attention spans; that is, it makes them more impulsive and less persevering. Once again, the effects appear to depend on the content viewed, and are not due to the medium itself. In one experiment, children were assigned to watch an hour of fast-paced programming or an hour of slow-paced programming. There were no effects on subsequent attention or perseverance (Anderson, Levin, & Lorch, 1977). In two studies over a longer period, children who watched typical children's programming showed reduced perseverance or increased impulsiveness (cf. Anderson & Collins, 1988). Conversely, children who watched the slow-paced *Mister Rogers' Neighborhood* became increasingly task persistent in their everyday activities in preschool (Friedrich & Stein, 1973).

The literature on television and cognitive processing was reviewed extensively for the U.S. Department of Education by Anderson and Collins (1988). Their conclusions are a good summary. While noting that the available research is sparse or, in many instances, of poor quality, they concluded that there is little evidence to support the idea that television as a medium has any effects on such cognitive processes as attention, creativity, impulsivity, or "attention span." By the same token, proposals that television may enhance spatial abilities or comprehension of filmic codes have yet to receive strong empirical support.

COGNITIVE PROCESSING OF TELEVISION

Rather than asking how television influences cognitive processes, we can ask how children process the medium. Approaching questions from this vantage point has been productive. There are extensive and precise investigations about attentional processes used during television viewing. Even very young children deploy their attention strategically rather than remaining glued to the screen most of the time. They look at and away from the set frequently, but not randomly or even simply in response to the patterns of noise and lights. From a very early age they make choices about what, when, and how attentively to watch. They may attend to vivid, rapidly moving images with audiovisual gimmicks and special effects, but such production features alone are not enough to maintain their interest for long (Huston & Wright, 1983; Wright & Huston, 1983). They attend to content they can understand (Anderson & Lorch, 1983) and to content that is funny or interesting (Bryant, Zillmann, & Brown, 1983). They think actively about what they are viewing, perhaps more than adults do.

Certain features of television programs do hold children's attention. They include humor, character movement, sound effects and auditory changes, children's and women's voices, and animation. Children tend to lose interest when programs contain men's voices, complex speech, live-animal photography, and long zooms (Alwitt, Anderson, Lorch, & Levin, 1980; Greer, Potts, Wright, & Huston, 1982; Huston & Wright, 1983). The most parsimonious explanation of these patterns is that the features that maintain attention are those that signal interesting and comprehensible content. For the most part, violence and aggression do not increase attention to a program that has other attractive features (Potts, Huston, & Wright, 1986). Although many children's programs, especially cartoons, contain high levels of violence, this violence is not necessary to hold children's interest; they like nonviolent programs with humor, animation, and other attention-getting features.

Comprehension

What children understand on television depends partly on their general level of cognitive development. Therefore, research on comprehension has a double payoff—it provides information about how children understand television and about more general developmental cognitive processes as well. Although children watch many programs designed for children, most of what they view is intended for adult audiences. The plots, characters, and situations they encounter are often unfamiliar to them. Until about age 9 or 10, they have difficulty understanding adult programs because they lack some needed cognitive skills or relevant information. For instance, a 7-year-old may have trouble following a story about a man who is trying to kill his ex-wife to prevent her from testifying against him because the child does not know what testimony and courts are.

Poor comprehension can also result from cognitive immaturity. Collins' 1983 work demonstrates, for example, that young children sometimes have difficulty discriminating central, important content from content that is tangential to the main point. An incidental sight gag (Fat Albert falling flat on his face, for instance) may seem at least as important as the central theme (two characters are trying to pursue activities that violate sex stereotypes). They may also fail to integrate different elements of a story that occur at different times. For example, a child may not connect the scene of a mugging in the subway with a later scene showing several men being arrested and taken to jail. Finally, they have difficulty making inferences about events that are not explicitly shown or about the feelings and intentions of characters. When the camera cuts from a scene in which two people are dining in a romantic setting to a bedroom with the morning light shining in, children do not infer the intervening events well.

PASSIVITY, INVOLVEMENT, AND EFFORT

Although television can present intellectual challenges, especially to young children, many people perceive it as a device to help them relax, disengage their brains, and let themselves be passively entertained. Adolescents and adults reported feeling more passive, uninvolved, relaxed, and unchallenged during television viewing than during many other activities. Heavy viewers generally reported feeling less happy, friendly, and positive than light viewers, but the causal direction is not clear. People who are unhappy and have difficulty filling unstructured time seem to seek the escape of television; whether television contributes further to their sense of discomfort is an open question (Kubey & Csikszentmihalyi, 1990).

One reason that viewers do not concentrate much mental effort on television is a widespread belief that television is "easy." When you watch television, you expect it to demand little so you relax and do not invest much effort in understanding it. That attitude is especially pervasive in the United States, where most programming is light entertainment, and it carries over to occasions when television could be used for learning. Salomon (1983) developed this line of thinking in a series of investigations that demonstrate the effects of invested mental effort. One intriguing study demonstrated that children in Israel learned more than American children did from an educational television program. Children from both nations learned equally well when the same content was presented in print. Apparently the American children concentrated less effort on television because they took it less seriously as a medium that demands some cognitive effort and as a source of useful information.

FORMS AND FORMATS

At a slightly different level, variations in pace, action, and production forms and formats within television influence viewing patterns. Television forms are visual and auditory features of the medium that are relatively independent of the content they are designed to convey. As children become sophisticated in the "language" of television (e.g., its codes for time and place changes and the uses of various production techniques) they can process what they see more thoroughly and learn more from it. Television forms can aid their understanding of program content in several ways: (1) by focusing attention on central or relevant content, (2) by signaling the type of content to be presented, (3) by carrying connotative meanings that enhance or clarify the content message, and (4) by eliciting participation and activity from the viewer.

As Collins (1983) demonstrated, young children often have difficulty selecting central content messages; they recall incidental content as well as central content from television programs. Formal features such as movement and sound effects can focus attention on central content so that children are more apt to recall it. For example, children recall central plot events better when the events are accompanied by an identifiable sound or visual effect (Calvert & Gersh, 1987; Calvert et al., 1982).

Media-wise children learn early that certain formal features signal certain types of content. Animation, peculiar voices, and sound effects are often used with child-oriented content that is funny, designed for children, and comprehensible. Adult male voices, low action, and talking heads are used with adult-oriented content that is uninteresting and incomprehensible to children. They not only attend to child-oriented cues more than to adult-oriented cues, but they learn more when content is packaged in such features. Television forms can lure children into doing some cognitive work when those forms signal that the content is age-appropriate, interesting, comprehensible, or otherwise worth some mental effort (Campbell, Wright, & Huston, 1987).

Some television forms carry connotative meanings, either because they resemble widely shared cultural symbols or because they are frequently associated with particular content on television. Rapid action, loud sound effects, and frequent cuts signify masculinity; background music, dissolves, and fuzzy images connote femininity (Welch, Huston-Stein, Wright, & Plehal, 1979). By about age 6, children recognize those sex-typed connotations even when the content is neutral (Huston, Greer, Wright, Welch, & Ross, 1984).

Form cues are also used to discriminate fictional from real events. Even young children distinguished footage of a real space launch from a program about a fictional spaceship (Leary, Wright, & Huston, 1985). Children who watched television coverage of the *Challenger* accident said that they knew it was real partly because of such form cues as print on the screen, poor quality video, long shots, the absence of close-ups of the astronauts, and disjointed speech by the announcers. All of these are very different from form cues used in space fiction (Wright, Kunkel, Pinon, & Huston, 1989).

Finally, forms and formats can partially overcome the so-called passive quality of television viewing. Children's programs such as *Pee Wee's Playhouse* elicit responses from home viewers by asking them to point, yell, and the like. Formats on *Sesame Street* and *The Electric Company* are designed to stimulate active processing. For example, a song is played once with the words sung, then the music is played without the words in a effort to get the home viewer to supply them (see Chapter 4).

SUMMARY

Does television displace other activities, change thought processes, and lead to passivity? The answers are mixed, but it is clear that the impact of television as a medium is not nearly as extreme or dramatic as its fondest proponents or its most virulent critics would have us think. Television does displace some activities, particularly those that are functionally similar to it. Although people's leisure-time activities change considerably when television is introduced, some of the displacement effects are dissipated over time, as the novelty of the medium wears off. People settle into a pattern of integrating the medium with other activities, which may represent a significant change from life without television, but the change is difficult to detect from the available data.

What impresses one most about the vast range of studies on cognitive processing is how limited the effects of the medium are. Television may have some slight influences on school achievement and reading, but both are much more clearly related to intelligence and to the social and environmental conditions that promote reading. It may affect creativity and imagination, but whether in a positive or negative direction is not clear. There is little evidence to support the notion that television per se leads to short attention spans or intellectual sloth.

Children process television actively, using whatever cognitive skills and knowledge they have. They deploy their attention actively and strategically to content that is comprehensible and interesting; they "turn off" when the program is beyond them or dull. They often fail to understand plot and story lines because of limitations in their ability to distinguish central plot information, integrate different portions of a plot, and draw inferences about implicit information. Their lack of knowledge about the adult world also leaves them bewildered about many events in the general-audience television that forms most of their viewing diet.

At the same time, children acquire an understanding of the conventions of the medium that helps them to select and comprehend content. They use such cues as animation to identify content appropriate for them, and they use formal cues to determine what is real and what is not. Judicious use of forms and formats can increase the amount children learn from educational programming. One barrier to using television for education, however, is that older children and adults treat television viewing as an occasion to relax and be passive, not to concentrate or exercise intensive mental effort. People in the United States are especially apt to believe that television is easy, in part because light entertainment programming predominates on American television. As a result, Americans exert less mental effort when presented with television than when they encounter print.

The Television-Viewing Environment

6

Psychologists and many others often concentrate on the messages of television and individual viewers' reactions to those messages. Yet, television viewing occurs in an environmental context that influences what and when viewing occurs as well as the ways in which viewers interpret what they see. Bryant and Anderson (1983) outlined the attributes of the individual and the environment that influence viewing. For most people most of the time, viewing occurs in the home. School environments may also indirectly influence children's viewing by providing assignments, suggestions, and training in media literacy. The television industry determines the viewing environment by deciding what types of programming and viewing options to supply. The larger society influences that environment through public policy regarding television and through economic forces affecting television broadcasting and technology.

In this chapter and the next, we consider some of these features of the viewing environment. We begin with the family, then discuss school media-literacy training. The impact of cable and new technologies is then considered. In Chapter 7, the economics of television and public policy are discussed.

PARENT MEDIATION IN THE HOME

Parents are the first and perhaps most important teachers about how to use television. Young children's viewing often occurs with parents. In a sample of 3- to 7-year-olds, the great majority (about

75%) of the time spent viewing adult programs was in the company of one or both parents. Older children have parents present less often when they watch entertainment fare, but children's early habits of television viewing depend greatly on the viewing patterns of their families (Lull, 1982). Both the amount viewed and the types of programs selected are influenced by their parents' examples. Hence, one important action that parents can take is to regulate their own viewing (Dorr, Kovaric, & Doubleday, 1989; St. Peters et al., in press).

Excessive or harmful television viewing is sometimes attributed to parental neglect or absence. Magazine articles regularly bemoan "latch-key" children parked in front of the television set because they are unsupervised. That belief is a myth. School-aged children whose parents are employed do not watch any more television than those whose parents (usually mothers) are at home after school (Messaris & Hornik, 1983). Preschoolers whose mothers are employed watch less television than those with full-time homemaker mothers (Pinon, Huston, & Wright, 1989), probably because they are in child-care settings where television is less available than it is at home. Children in child care may also have more alternatives to television than children at home because there are always playmates available and there is often a wide range of toys and activities.

One reason parental absence does not increase children's television viewing is that parents who are present rarely restrict children's viewing. Survey studies of children in middle childhood and adolescence have demonstrated repeatedly that most parents do not regulate their children's television viewing. In a longitudinal study of children from ages 3 to 7, however, the majority of parents said they prohibited the viewing of some types of programs. Violence and sexual content were the most frequent reasons for the restrictions, but the programs involved were most often R-rated films on cable or videotape. Most parents did not discourage the viewing of cartoons, crime shows, and other violent programs on broadcast television. Similarly, most parents did not limit the total viewing time of these young children.

Parents' restrictions on violent and sexual content are likely to protect children from some harmful effects. However, there is also some evidence suggesting that limitations on time might produce beneficial consequences. Heavy-television viewers (four hours a day or more) expend less effort on school work, have poorer reading skills, play less well with friends, and have fewer hobbies and activities than light viewers. Although it is not clear whether television viewing causes these outcomes or is partly a result of them, parental intervention may encourage children to spend more of their time more profitably. If a child often chooses to watch television rather than play with friends, talks only about television programs and characters, or is not performing well in school, a parent may decide to cut back on the amount of time the youngster spends in front of the television set. In one experimental study, parents limited viewing time for 6-year-olds to about half their normal amount. In comparison to an unrestricted control group, children whose viewing was limited showed improvement in certain types of cognitive performance and increased the amount of time they spent reading (Gadberry, 1980).

Some parents encourage children to watch programs that the parents consider beneficial—educational shows, nature documentaries, and children's specials. Parents who both encourage and restrict viewing are selective; they are also more likely to watch television with their children than those who do not. Not surprisingly, parents who have positive attitudes about television watch with their children more than those who do not (Dorr et al., 1989). The children most at risk are those whose parents neither encourage nor regulate their viewing; such children watch a considerable amount of adult-entertainment television and are apt to view without an adult present (Wright, St. Peters, & Huston, 1990).

Parental viewing with children (coviewing) can enhance many of the positive outcomes of television viewing and reduce some of the negative influences. Adult coviewers can increase the amount children learn from educational programs (Salomon, 1977) and help children understand plot elements (Collins, Sobol, & Westby, 1981; Watkins, Calvert, Huston-Stein, & Wright,

1980). They can also counteract some of the negative effects of violence and antisocial content by expressing their disapproval, pointing out that the content is not appropriate to real life, and discussing nonviolent values with their children (Greenberg, 1972; Huesmann, Eron, Klein, Brice, & Fischer, 1983).

Although parents can teach, preach, and discuss television when they watch with their children, there is little evidence that they actually do so in everyday circumstances. Most of the programs that children watch with their parents are general-audience programs. When preschool children watch programs designed for children, their parents are present 25% of the time or less (Field, 1989; Wright et al., 1990). Parents do not often take advantage of the opportunity to enhance the effects of *Sesame Street*, for example. Moreover, the amount of time spent coviewing does not predict children's performance on a variety of intellectual tasks (e.g., measures of vocabulary) or even on tests measuring how well television is understood (e.g., what is fiction and what is real) (Dorr et al., 1989; Field, 1989; St. Peters, Fitch, Wright, & Huston, 1989). School-aged children whose parents watch television with them often are more apt to consider television as a source of learning than children with low frequencies of coviewing (Dorr et al., 1989). But many parents do not take full advantage of the opportunity to share ideas and views with their children when they watch television together.

There are several good sources of information and advice to help parents select and plan their children's television use. In Table 6.1, several suggestions to parents are offered. Action for Children's Television publishes materials for parents, and such books as *Taking Advantage of Media: A Manual for Parents and Teachers* (Brown, 1986) provide useful ideas and suggestions. These books contrast with the antitelevision views of Winn (1987) and others. Rather than recommending that parents eliminate television, they provide information about how to take advantage of its positive offerings and how to reduce some of its negative effects. Such a stand is consistent with the theme of this book—that television can make both positive and negative contributions to

Table 6.1 Suggestions for Parents

REGULATING TIME WITH TV
● Keep a time chart with the child of his or her activities, including TV viewing, homework, and play with friends. Discuss with the child what to eliminate and what to put in its place.
● Set a weekly viewing limit. Have the child select programs from television schedules at the beginning of the week. Parents can assign points to programs and give the child a point total to spend weekly. Programs that a parent does not want the child to watch can "cost" more in points.
● Rule out TV at certain times, such as before breakfast or on school nights.
● Make a list of alternative activities—riding a bicycle, reading a book, working on a hobby. Before watching TV, the child must choose and do something from the list.
● Encourage the entire family to have a program choice in mind before turning the TV set on and to turn it off when the show they planned to watch is over.
● Remember that you set an example for your child. If you watch a lot of TV, chances are your child will also.

COPING WITH VIOLENCE
● Watch at least one episode of the programs the child watches to know how violent they are.
● When viewing TV together, discuss the violence with the child. Talk about why the violence happened and how painful it is. Ask the child how conflict can be solved without violence.
● Explain to the child how violence on an entertainment program is "faked."
● Encourage children to watch programs with characters that cooperate, help, and care for each other. These programs have been shown to influence children in a positive way.

APPLYING TELEVISION TO REAL LIFE
● Ask children to compare what they see on the screen with people, places, and events they know firsthand, have read about, or studied in school.

Table 6.1 (Continued)

● Encourage children to read newspapers, listen to the radio, talk to adults about their work, or meet people from different ethnic or social backgrounds.

● Tell children what is real and what is make-believe on TV. Explain how television uses stunt people, camera zooms, dream sequences, and animation to create fantasy.

● Explain to the child the values your family holds about sex, alcohol, and drugs.

UNDERSTANDING ADVERTISING

● Tell children that the purpose of advertising is to sell products to as many viewers as possible.

● Put advertising disclaimers into words children understand: e.g., "Partial assembly required" means "you have to put it together before you can play with it."

● On shopping trips, let children see the toys that look big, fast, and exciting on the screen, but that look disappointingly small and slow close-up.

● Teach the child a few facts about nutrition and then let him or her use them. For example, if the youngster can read package labels, allow the child to choose the breakfast cereal from those in which sugar is not one of the first ingredients listed.

children and to society. It is not inherently evil or destructive to children—the effects of television depend on how it is used.

MEDIA-LITERACY TRAINING

Parents are potentially the most important influence on children's television viewing, but teachers and educational activities can have a similar, if less omnipresent role.

School Curricula
Television programs and the topic of television itself have been used as a "media-literacy" curriculum in some public schools, in

an attempt to teach children to be careful consumers and to moderate the potentially negative effects of programs. In a project for third, fourth, and fifth graders, Singer, Singer, and Zuckerman (1981b) developed eight lesson plans to be used as part of the social studies curriculum in a suburban school. Twice a week for four weeks, the children watched videotapes that had been developed for the classroom, and the teachers discussed the content, with guidance from the lesson plans that they had been trained to use.

The topics of these lessons included the electronics of television; the different types of television programs; the difference between reality and fantasy on television; the purpose of commercials; the effects of television on the viewers' knowledge, attitudes, and feelings (including prejudice); the ways that violence is portrayed on television; and the ways that viewers can control their own television habits and attempt to influence the networks' programs. In addition, the curriculum used topics relevant to television programs to teach critical-thinking skills, art, and language skills, with projects such as summarizing the plot of a program that they had watched, or drawing pictures depicting alternative strategies for coping with anger in a program that was violent. Each lesson lasted 40 to 50 minutes and included possible homework assignments.

For example, in the lesson dealing with violence on television, the teacher asked the children to name any shows that they had seen during the previous week that had violence in them, and the teacher wrote these programs on the board. Children were asked to define aggression and were taught the difference between being assertive and being aggressive. The causes and effects of violence were also discussed, along with the ways they were portrayed in the programs. Teachers also asked the children if they had ever imitated the violence they saw on television.

In the lesson on prejudice and stereotypes, the children were asked to describe the kinds of people who were portrayed unrealistically in television programs, including the handicapped, minorities, and men and women of different ages and occupations. Possible homework assignments included being a "stereotype detective" by looking for stereotypic characters on commercials and programs, or drawing pictures of people in nontraditional roles. The impact of the curriculum was assessed by testing the children several weeks before and after the four-week curriculum, as well as three months later. The results showed that the children made significant short-term and long-term gains in understanding the words and concepts that were taught, such as prejudice, animation, aggression, and advertisement (Singer, Zuckerman, & Singer, 1980).

The curriculum developed for this study was revised and made available in a book for teachers, entitled *Getting the Most Out of T.V.* (Singer, Singer, & Zuckerman, 1981a). In addition, ABC-TV used the materials presented in the videotapes to make a commercial program.

In a project that used already existing television programs with preschool children, the teachers' classroom discussions following the children's viewing of regular prosocial television programs increased the children's learning of words and concepts that were included in the program (Singer et al., 1981b). In a similar study, adults read storybooks summarizing important concepts after children viewed a prosocial television program; children understood these concepts and were able to generalize them to new situations better than those who had watched without the storybook summary (Friedrich & Stein, 1975).

These projects show that teachers can use videotapes and the topics of television to teach words and concepts to children ranging in age from 4 to 10. The teachers can use existing prosocial programs or can go beyond the programs available and talk about topics such as prejudice, violence, and reality, using television programs that are not necessarily designed for educational purposes.

Teaching about Advertising
Other media-literacy curricula have included efforts to teach children about advertising as part of a larger body of instruction (Dorr, Graves, & Phelps, 1980; Lloyd-Kolkin, Wheeler, & Strand, 1980; Singer et al., 1980). Some curricula have been devoted entirely to

advertising (S. Feshbach, N. D. Feshbach, & Cohen, 1983; Roberts, Christenson, Gibson, Mooser, & Goldberg, 1980). Children as young as 4 can be taught to identify commercials and to understand their general purpose. However, it is not clear that increased knowledge induces skepticism about commercials or affects subsequent consumer behavior. In one study of elementary and preschool children, skepticism increased and desire for products declined, but simulated purchase choices were not affected in preschoolers and kindergarten children (S. Feshbach et al., 1983). In another, both second and sixth graders' ratings of advertised products were lower after the children saw films designed to teach consumer skills (Roberts et al., 1980). Television can be used to teach about advertising. Public-service announcements about commercials can increase children's awareness of the persuasive intent of advertising and decrease belief in the truthfulness of advertisements, but they do not influence the appeal of advertised products (Christenson, 1982). However, industry attempts to use this approach have been minimal and not especially effective (Dorr, Doubleday, Kovaric, & Kunkel, 1981).

Summary

Parents can help their children to use television wisely by regulating their children's viewing in two ways—restricting objectionable programs and encouraging positive programs—and by regulating their own viewing. Parents are crucial models for the amount and kinds of programs children watch. They can help children to understand and evaluate television content in ways that may diminish some of its negative effects, and they can enhance its positive effects by selecting and discussing beneficial programs. That parents can and should guide their children's viewing does not relieve the television industry and public policymakers from their responsibility to ensure that television offerings are diverse and free of clearly harmful content.

School curricula can also be successful in teaching children about television production and advertising. Such curricula help children to understand television and be skeptical about advertising, but we need considerably more information about how to make the curricula effective influences on children's viewing behavior. Future research in this domain could be fruitful.

NEW TECHNOLOGIES

A child of our acquaintance, who is not quite 3 years old, watches *Sesame Street* in the mornings. She does not, however, watch a regular broadcast because her local station does not carry it at the time her parents are getting ready for work. They record it each day, and she watches the tape with remote control in hand. When she likes a bit, she replays it three or four times; when she docs not like a bit, she presses "fast forward" and zips through it. Her mother says she occasionally gets upset when she watches broadcast television and cannot go back and forth at will in the program.

This child lives in a different technological environment than her peers did five or ten years ago. Television is no longer just what is broadcast on the airwaves. In the United States, television is no longer restricted to broadcasts by a few large companies. Today the average viewer has access to numerous program channels supplied by cable, including specialized pay-cable stations (e.g., HBO, Disney, Univision). In addition, viewers own or can rent videotape recorders to watch their choice of tapes whenever they like.

Children and adults are exposed to different types of programs on cable than on commercial television. Some of this content is positive (e.g., educational and cultural programs), but some of it is potentially harmful (e.g., graphic violence). Videotapes allow access to material that would not otherwise be available via commercial television, cinema, and perhaps even cable. Consequently, when we consider such issues as violence, sex and sexual violence, sex roles, minorities, health, family relations, and other topics, it is essential to take into account the media individuals are using beyond broadcast television.

To date there has been little research focused directly on the effects of exposure to cable or videotapes. Do people watch television differently, for example, with these technologies? Do they watch more or different types of programs? Most of the research has concerned itself with the diffusion of these new media and with their content.

Spread of New Technologies

In the forecasts of the 1970s about the impact of technological change, few even noticed the advent of the humble remote control. Yet, by the late 1980s, more than 75% of American households had remote controls (Dorr & Kunkel, 1990). Viewing patterns reportedly changed. People not only turn off the advertisements, but switch rapidly from program to program in a pattern sometimes called grazing. Some people watch two or three programs simultaneously, trying to catch just enough of each to keep up with the story (Dorr & Kunkel, 1990).

In the 1970s and 1980s cable television grew rapidly; its greater channel capacity permitted "narrow-casting," providing programs designed to meet the needs of specialized audiences, including children and minorities. Cable transmission is supported by a combination of advertising and user fees. Just over half the homes in the country (54.8%) now subscribe to cable (Dorr & Kunkel, 1990). However, cable availability is skewed toward the affluent because of cost and because many rural and low-income urban areas are not served by any cable company.

In the last few years, home videotape recorders have enjoyed enormously rapid diffusion. In 1989, it was estimated that 60–65% of United States households had a videotape recorder, and many predict that ownership will climb to between 75% and 85% before leveling off (Dorr & Kunkel, 1990). For those who do not own a player, almost every supermarket offers inexpensive rentals. Children in other countries also have increasing access to videorecorders (Greenberg, Linsangan, & Soderman, 1987).

Interactive television has been available in some forms for almost 20 years, but has not yet received widespread use. There were local experiments with interactive television in the 1970s. The most widely known was the QUBE system in Columbus, Ohio. Viewers could respond to opinion polls or other questions using a set of numbered buttons. In 1987, an interactive program was introduced to children's television. A signal was transmitted with the program that would activate a computerized toy (to be purchased separately); viewers could shoot at targets in the program or at each others' toys. It is unclear at present whether that use of interactive technology will be repeated in other commercial programs because it was not a large commercial success. It is unfortunate that the first use of interactive television for children was devoted to making them active participants in war-based scenarios. The technology has the potential for powerful positive uses, particularly in children's educational programs.

Programs on Cable and Videotape

Cable channels do expand the number and range of offerings. Even a modest 17-channel cable service provides sufficient variety that a viewer can choose from comedy, drama, news, action adventure, and variety shows during most time slots (Huston et al., 1990). Cable supplies specialized programming for some demographic minorities—namely children, blacks, Hispanics, and some other ethnic or nationality groups. Nickelodeon, the Disney Channel, and a few other cable channels broadcast a considerable amount of children's programming, some of it informative (Siemicki, Atkin, Greenberg, & Baldwin, 1986). For example, in 1983, Disney carried 22 hours of children's informational programs and over 50 hours of general entertainment for children per week (Kerkman, Huston, Wright, & Eakins, 1990). The entertainment programs on children's cable channels are fairly diverse and include game shows, movie reviews, and children's dramas. Cable also supplies music videos, which are popular with children and young adults. In most metropolitan areas, there are cable channels in languages other than English—Spanish, Chinese, and the like. However, cable channels are available only in homes subscribing to cable services for a monthly fee; some channels, such as Disney require an additional fee beyond basic cable. Therefore, there may be serious inequities in access to cable for low-income groups.

Videotapes should also allow greater diversity than broadcast television, but in this early stage of their development it is not clear that they do. In one survey of children's videos available for rental, there was no more diversity than in broadcast television (Wartella, Heintz, Aidman, & Mazzarella, 1990). Most videotapes are movies originally produced for theaters or television.

Cable and videotapes provide access to far more graphic violence and explicit sex than does broadcast television. Recent studies have indicated that children with videotape recorders and/or cable access have seen more R-rated films than their counterparts without such access. Many of these films would not be shown on commercial television, or if shown, the violence and sex would be cut. Children are being exposed to much different materials today than in the past. More graphic violence, sexual content, and "mature themes" are readily available for everyone. For example, in music videos, 50% contain at least one occurrence of violence, a rate that far exceeds that of commercial television.

Use of Cable and Videotapes

One might expect increased viewing with cable because of the greater number and diversity of offerings. It appears that viewing increases some with cable, but it is often difficult to determine cause and effect. People with cable watch more than those without it, but they may have subscribed because they are more fond of television than those who do not choose to spend their money on a cable subscription. Viewing patterns shift when cable supplies greater diversity. For example, children watched more cartoons when they received weekday cartoons on cable than when they were limited to the weekend offerings of the network affiliate stations (Huston et al., 1990).

Videotape recorders appear to supplement broadcast television rather than replace it. Surveys of children and adolescents demonstrate that they use videotape recorders regularly, but such use does not replace broadcast television. Adolescents use VCRs primarily to watch movies, not to time-shift broadcast programs (Morgan, Alexander, Shanahan, & Harris, 1990). Children watch videocassettes regularly, but not for large amounts of time. In one study, 20 children were observed watching *Sesame Street* cassettes. Because their parents did not allow the children to touch the equipment, children watched the tapes without replaying or fast-forwarding. They typically watched cassettes about an hour a week (Rice & Sell, 1990).

Assessing the impact of new technology requires aiming at a rapidly moving target. People adapt to new technologies gradually; therefore, the changes in their viewing are probably gradual, too. As VCRs become routine pieces of household television equipment, children and adults probably discover new ways to use them and overcome initial fears and inhibitions. The children whom Rice and Sell observed did not use the VCR to its full advantage because their parents still considered VCR viewing a special activity that required negotiation and arrangements. In a few years, some of these parents will probably treat the VCR more casually, and they may be more willing to allow children the freedom to use it.

There are a lot of unanswered questions about the effects of cable and VCRs on children and adults. The area is ripe for good research. We need more information about how such technologies affect the viewing process. Using a remote control and a videotape to repeat or replay information, skip dull parts, and the like could make television viewing a more active and stimulating learning process. Perhaps grazing or simultaneous viewing of several programs teaches people to "time share" their attention, or perhaps it teaches them to fragment it. We need good research to explore the issue.

The content of cable and videotapes also raises new questions about influences on children. Given our theoretical understanding of the influences of media factors such as violence, gender roles, affect, and formal features, we might anticipate even more pronounced effects of cable and videotape content than the content on broadcast television.

SUMMARY

Children begin learning about how to use television at home. Parents play a crucial role in socializing viewing habits, largely through their own use of television. Parents also influence children's viewing by encouraging children to watch good programs and regulating what and how much television their children watch. When parents watch television with their children, they can use the opportunity to help children learn or to counteract negative messages. However, the evidence to date suggests that parents do not take full advantage of the opportunities afforded by coviewing. That parents can and should guide their children's viewing does not relieve the television industry and public policymakers of their responsibility to ensure that television offerings are diverse and free of clearly harmful content.

Once children reach elementary school, they have a long history of exposure to television. Nevertheless, schools can teach children media literacy. Several organized programs have been successful in teaching children to distinguish fiction from reality on television and to understand the economics of television and advertising. It is less clear that such programs affect viewing patterns, and we need considerably more information about how to make them effective influences on children's viewing behavior.

The technological changes in television have produced changes in viewing patterns for adults and children. Remote controls, cable, and videotape recorders are all available in the majority of American homes. Cable supplies a wider range of programs than broadcast television and permits narrow-casting to specialized audiences. The supply of programs for children and ethnic minorities has been increased as a result. Home videotape players allow the use of a wide variety of programming, though what is currently available is not more diverse than broadcast television. They release the viewer from scheduling constraints of other forms of television and they provide opportunities for active viewing because they allow a viewer to repeat or skip sections and schedule viewing. Because there are few if any restraints on the content of most cable channels or videotapes, they contain much more graphic violence and explicit sex than broadcast television. Children are watching such programs in larger amounts than they did before these technologies were available.

New technologies have the potential for allowing positive uses of television that should be exploited. In-school instructional television is increasing, in part because programs are available on videotape, and teachers can schedule them at their convenience. Videotapes permit the viewer to control pace and repetition individually. Changing technologies also raise new problems of negative influences that require not only research, but innovative thinking about public policy that may protect vulnerable populations from harmful effects.

Economics of Television
and Public Policy

Economic, political, and social forces in a society ultimately shape the media environment available to its citizens. The nations of the world have vastly different television as well as wide variations in newspapers, books, radio, and other media. Their differences arise from the diverse political systems and values that in turn shape government policies and from differing economic bases for the production and distribution of media. Economic forces are particularly important in the television industry because, by comparison to print media or radio, television programming is much more expensive to produce and distribute.

In many parts of the world, the mass media are virtually an arm of the government, and their content is determined by the social and political objectives of that government. Even countries in which multiple political parties have a voice and where a fair amount of freedom of expression is permitted vary considerably in how much the government controls, finances, and organizes television. Perhaps the most important distinction is commercial versus public funding of production and distribution.

COMMERCIAL VERSUS PUBLIC FUNDING

"Television" is in fact a diverse set of technologies provided through a variety of economic and technological arrangements. In the United States, television has been financed primarily as a private commercial enterprise since its inception; in many other nations, including virtually all of western Europe, television is publicly financed and controlled.

The scope and diversity of television programming varies with the economic basis and the organizational structure of the broadcasting system. The major dimensions differentiating broadcasting structures are ownership and control. Whether the ownership of transmission and production facilities is vested in the public or private sectors and whether the control exercised by various agencies is extensive or minimal, formal or informal, profoundly influences the quantity and quality of programming available. Both within and across nations, publicly funded programming is typically more informative and better tailored to the needs of various ethnic and demographic minorities than commercially funded programs (Kippax & Murray, 1979).

The nature of television and the context in which such major issues as violence and advertising are defined can be understood by examining the historical and geographical influences that have shaped the broadcasting systems in various countries. The United States is almost alone in the world in giving preference to developing television as a commercial medium rather than as a public service. Most other countries began their television broadcasting as a public or government-owned and supported medium that did not give licenses to private owners. Most other countries also take television more seriously than we do in the United States; governments, private institutions, and citizens see television as an important medium to be used for general education and information. It is only secondarily an entertainment medium and a means of selling goods and services (Melody, 1973; Murray & Kippax, 1981; Rowland, 1983).

In the Scandinavian countries, Denmark, Norway, and Sweden, for instance, television is controlled by governments that hold a monopoly on broadcasting. There is no advertising, and television-broadcast time is generally restricted to about 50 hours per week. There is a strong emphasis on educational and informational programs and a consistently high standard of quality entertainment programs. In Finland a similar picture emerges, although there is mixed private and government ownership of media, and limited advertising is allowed.

In other Western European countries, Austria, France, Italy, Switzerland, and West Germany, there is monopoly control of television either by government-licensed private companies, as in Switzerland, or by government-funded independent broadcast authorities. Broadcast time in these systems is generally restricted to about 70 hours per week, and morning broadcasts are devoted to educational and school programs. In some cases there is very limited advertising, whereas in other cases more time is devoted to advertising, but none of these broadcasting systems is very dependent on revenue from advertising. The programming appears to be slightly "lighter" than that in the Scandinavian countries, but in each country special attention is given to minority audiences and informational and educational programs.

In all of these broadcast systems, there are only one or two channels (with the exception of France, with three channels), and broadcast time is somewhat restricted. However, in the United Kingdom, there is no monopolistic ownership of television broadcasting. Of the four channels, two are publicly owned and two are commercially operated. The average viewing time available is longer in England than in the other countries described (broadcasting time is about 90 hours per week). While the BBC carries educational, information and quality entertainment programs, the commercial IBA network generally broadcasts lighter fare. However, both the second BBC channel and the second IBC channel have a mandate to provide programming for numerically small audiences who are not well served by more popular programs.

In three other countries, which share some political and cultural characteristics with England—Australia, Canada, and the United States—again there is no monopoly ownership of television. However, in these countries there is a much heavier emphasis on commercial broadcasting than is the case in England. All three countries broadcast more hours per week on more channels than any of the previously described systems. Furthermore, the commercial stations in these countries carry more advertising than many of the other countries. As both Australia and Canada import many of their programs from the United States, there is considerable similarity in the programming available in all three countries. In general, it would be fair to say that, although all three countries have a public, government-supported television system, the national television character is primarily distinguished by the commercial television systems that broadcast programming designed primarily for light entertainment.

Programming in the United States and Britain "trickles down" to many poorer nations throughout the world. The broadcasting systems in many Latin American countries, for example, are similar in structure to the United States' system of privately owned stations. Even government-owned systems in poor countries often depend heavily on advertising revenues. Moreover, because television is so expensive to produce, the majority of programs in many of these countries are imported, most often from the United States or Britain. Unfortunately, many of the imports represent the worst rather than the best of United States television.

Is there any relationship between these various broadcasting structures and the nature of the programming for children and other specialized audiences? The answer is: emphatically, yes. In countries where the broadcasting structure is based on advertising revenues, both the quantity and the quality of programming available to children are problematic. We have already noted that in the United States there are similar issues about programming serving the elderly, minorities, and women. In other nations, the demand for advertising revenues may inhibit indigenous programming. In Jamaica, for example, a widely acclaimed local production was discontinued because of lack of advertiser support; advertisers were convinced that they received larger audiences with the imported fare that dominated the broadcast schedule of the government-owned network.

Chief among the causes of the neglect of minority audiences is that the commercial television system must generate revenue through programming that attracts large, heterogeneous, affluent audiences. The broadcaster is caught in the dilemma of providing programs for a diverse audience, at reasonable cost, with a reasonable return on the investment. Some media observers have charged that this is the major flaw in the American broadcasting structure: "Television is largely entertainment designed with the motive of assembling as many viewers of commercial interest to advertisers as possible. No other aspiration, restraint, or inhibition significantly affects the process of program design" (Comstock, 1980, p.3).

Industry representatives have countered by charging that Comstock has oversimplified the issue and that the industry "genuinely aspires to be a mass medium" (Milavsky, 1980, p.5). Milavsky also notes that the present American television system is a direct result of the Federal Communications Act of 1934, which "consciously and deliberately intended to ensure that broadcasting be free of governmental influence. That is why it is totally dependent on advertiser revenue, as opposed to direct taxes or license fees" (p.5). In passing, one cannot avoid the observation that Milavsky leans toward oversimplification—just as there is no such thing as a free lunch, there is no such thing as free television. As Gerbner (1980) has remarked: "The advertising subsidy that supports and guides the cultural industry is extracted through a levy on the price of all advertised goods and services. Some call this private taxation without representation. The tax is hidden in the price of soap; I pay when I wash, not when I watch." (p.2). And there's the rub—a commercial television structure dependent on mass audiences seems unable to provide adequate and necessary programming for small but important audiences.

Public and commercial broadcasting systems do provide significantly different types of programming. As an example, one week of broadcasting on public and commercial stations in England, Australia, and the United States in the late 1970s is shown in Table 7.1. The information is illuminating because it confirms the long-held suspicion that those who are poor or small—in number or stature—are ill-served by commercial television. And, although this is true across the three continents, it is less true in England. When these data were assembled, the public station in Australia devoted 47% of its weekly broadcast time to educational and children's shows, in contrast to only 8% on the commercial station. Similarly, in the United States the public station committed

Table 7.1 Percentage of Time Devoted to Different Program
Types during One Week of Public and Commercial Television
Programming in England, Australia, and the United States

Program Category	England[a]			Australia[b]		United States[c]	
	Publ.	Publ.	Com.	Publ.	Com.	Publ.	Com.
News & Public Affairs	24.5	12.0	13.0	13.8	5.2	22.5	14.0
Features or Documentaries	6.5	20.0	6.3	8.1	2.1	6.0	.5
Education	23.0	29.5	12.5	26.3	.4	26.0	2.0
Arts & Music	1.0	2.5	—	2.1	—	5.0	—
Children's Programs	11.5	6.5	8.0	20.8	7.5	27.0	4.0
Drama (plays)	4.5	4.5	3.1	2.8	—	—	—
Drama (series/serials)	7.0	4.0	16.6	9.8	24.5	5.0	17.0
Movies	6.5	11.0	12.0	3.2	33.3	5.5	18.0
General Entertainment	7.5	7.5	9.5	3.8	17.8	—	24.5
Sports	6.0	1.5	6.2	8.4	6.1	2.0	4.5
Religion	1.0	—	.6	1.1	3.0	—	.5

Note: From *Television and Youth: 25 Years of Research and Controversy*
(p.66) by J. P. Murray, 1980, Boys Town, NE: Boys Town Center for the Study
of Youth and Development. Reprinted by permission of author. Percentages do
not always total 100% because some programs were not classified.
a. Data collected in March 1973. The public channels are BBC-1 and BBC-2.
The commercial channel is Anglia.
b. Data collected in April 1978. The public station is ABC-2. The commercial
station is TEN-10. Both stations are in Sydney.
c. Data collected in March 1973. The public station is KQED. The commercial
station is Channel 7. Both stations are in San Francisco.

53% of its time to children's and educational programs, compared
with only a 6% commitment by its commercial counterpart. In
England, BBC1 devoted 34% and BBC2 added 36% of its broadcasting time to the children's and educational areas, but the first
commercial station also devoted more than 20% to these areas.

According to two content analyses of United States television
in the 1980s, these patterns did not change for the better; in fact,
they became more pronounced. In the period from 1981 to 1985,

commercial networks averaged less than one hour per week of informative children's programming; independent channels in the United States had slightly higher levels—four hours per week. Public television provided 27 hours per week of informative children's programs (Kerkman et al., 1990; Phillips, Williams, & Travis, 1986).

Why is there this continental drift between the public and commercial stations in the United States and Australia in contrast to the more complementary relationship between the public and commercial systems in England? One possible answer lies in the second dimension of structure proposed above—the amount of regulation or control by the public. In England, television broadcasting began as a public instrumentality devoted to public rather than private service. It was only many years later that the commercial system, the IBA, came into being. By that time, the notion that the nation's screens should carry substance in addition to soap had become firmly implanted in the minds of the British viewer. Not so in the West or the South. In the New and Antipodean worlds the commercial system was the dominant force in determining the nature of television programming. The result is a television environment in the United States and, to a lesser extent, in Australia that is less than optimal for the developing child and other specialized audiences.

PUBLIC POLICY

The United States is almost alone in the world in having no clear public policy about television. The major legislation governing television is the Communications Act of 1934, which requires that television stations serve the "public interest, convenience, and necessity," and its enforcement has typically been minimal. We as a society are reluctant to formulate government policies, partly because television is defined as the province of private commercial interests and partly because the tradition of the First Amendment virtually precludes government intervention in program content.

Nevertheless, government agencies make decisions that affect the nature of television; those decisions ought to be based on an articulated set of principles. Two primary goals appear reasonable: (1) to promote quality, diverse programming that serves the needs of the many groups in our society, and (2) to protect citizens against harmful effects (Huston, Watkins, & Kunkel, 1989).

The major policy battles in the United States have been fought over programming for children (cf. Huston et al., 1989; Kunkel & Watkins, 1987). Because children are particularly vulnerable and malleable, both citizen-advocates and industry apologists acknowledge the importance of protecting and serving them. Government intervention on behalf of any of the other groups of concern in this book (i.e., ethnic minorities, women, or the elderly) has been rare, even though some legal basis exists for such intervention. It could be argued that government agencies have responsibility for ensuring that television meets the needs of a wide range of citizen groups, but such requirements are seldom considered in policy discussions or legislation.

The policy debates over children's programming are a microcosm of basic policy dilemmas in the United States. On the one hand various citizen groups have been increasingly vocal in pressing their demands for more and better programs for children. Action for Children's Television, for example, has argued repeatedly that airing commercially unprofitable programming for children is part of the "price" each station should pay in return for the grant of a broadcasting license. For its part, the industry claims that children are an important and special audience but the costs of providing quality programming are prohibitive. Many of the possible resolutions of this dilemma involve some basic structural changes in the nature of children's television.

Evidence like that shown in Table 7.1 makes it clear that having an economic base for children's programming is critical for restructuring. In the absence of pressure to obtain advertisers for particular programs, the constraints on the production of children's educational programming are moderated. This leads to the inescapable conclusion that one way out of the current stalemate is to reduce the pressure of market forces on the nature of children's television.

Although the problems in programming for children have been evident for many years, few changes in children's television have occurred. Industry representatives have maintained that changes in the diversity and quality of programming for special audiences should be brought about voluntarily by the television networks with encouragement from codes established by industry representatives (such as the National Association of Broadcasters). Voluntary guidelines might be preferable to government regulation, but they have not succeeded.

In 1974, for example, the Federal Communications Commission made explicit a policy that each broadcaster was required to make a meaningful effort to provide programming for children. They identified several deficiencies in available programming: there were too few informative programs, age-specific programs were lacking, children's programs were concentrated in weekend time slots, and the amount of advertising to children was excessive. They agreed, however, to allow the industry time to remedy these deficiencies.

In 1979, the FCC Children's Television Task Force evaluated the broadcasters' progress in dealing with the concerns identified five years earlier. They concluded that there were virtually no changes in the number of informative, age-specific programs, or the scheduling of children's programming. There was some reduction in advertising. Nevertheless, the FCC did not take regulatory action. They decided that "marketplace forces" and the increasing channel capacity represented by cable might bring about the needed changes in children's programs. As we noted in Chapter 6, cable has indeed expanded the range and scheduling of offerings for children, but broadcast television has not moved in the direction envisioned by the FCC.

The political climate of deregulation in the 1980s led to removal of the few existing regulations regarding children's television. For instance, restrictions on the amount of time devoted to advertising were rescinded; as a result, advertising began to increase. Moreover, product-related programs almost took over children's hours on commercial stations (Kunkel, 1988b). The FCC also removed the requirement that each broadcaster must serve children's needs; instead, it was sufficient if children's programming was available somewhere in the market area.

If the public becomes sufficiently concerned about children's television in the 1990s, the FCC may once again move toward more regulation. However, it is clear that the FCC does not act independently of Congress or the administration in power. It can be prodded into action at times, but it cannot be the leader in changing the structure of programs for children or other groups. The Congress, the executive branch, the courts, and private citizens all contribute to policies that produce change.

Regulatory Legislation
Although Congress obviously cannot legislate the specific content of television programs, it can set general requirements that broadcasters offer informative, educational programming for children. In 1990, Congress passed the Children's Television Education Act, after several years of unsuccessful efforts by its proponents. The bill became law without President Bush's signature. It requires licensees to demonstrate at the time of license renewal that they have provided programming to meet the educational and informational needs of children and youth. The bill does not set specific requirements for the number of hours of such programming that must be provided nor does it require age-specific programming for preschool and elementary school-aged children. Moreover, there are questions about how effectively it will be implemented and enforced by a Federal Communications Commission that continues to resist regulatory activity. However, it is the first such legislation in the 40 years of television broadcasting in this country. It establishes the principle that broadcasters have a social responsibility to their child audiences. The advantage to the approach used in this legislation is that it avoids the thorny issues of censorship. It specifies a positive requirement that programming meet the needs of children rather than a restriction on what may be broadcast.

Australia has a requirement that stations devote a time slot each day to informative programs for children. Programs are selected by a board composed of professionals and citizen-advocates. The requirement has been under siege in recent years, but it was quite effective in promoting production and distribution of quality programs for children.

A second legislative direction is regulation of advertising. The Children's Television Education Act contains limits on the amount of time that may be devoted to advertising during programming for which children are the primary audience. The limits however, are less stringent that those that were in force in FCC regulations before 1983—not more than 10 1/2 minutes per hour on Saturday morning and 12 minutes per hour on weekdays. These regulations leave time for many advertisements on children's television, but it is important that Congress established the principle that legal regulation is appropriate.

The Children's Television Education Act also dealt with the issue of product-related programming. The Federal Communications Commission was instructed to propose a ruling on program-length commercials. At the very least, the legislation provides a forum for examining the problem and a basis for legal action by citizen groups and other interested parties.

Still another successful legislative effort passed in 1990 is designed to promote self-regulation in the industry by removing antitrust restraints on collaboration among networks. The antitrust laws prohibit broadcasters or networks from forming an industrywide code to reduce violence or other objectional content because such cooperation is legally defined as restraint of trade. The newly passed law permits, but does not require, industry collaboration (including cable companies) to reduce violent content.

Funding for Quality Programs

The economic facts are simple: If commercial, profit-oriented funding does not generate quality programs, then some other source of funds is needed. One major step that the government could and should take is to restore the cuts and increase funding for production and distribution of informative programming. Public funds from a variety of sources provided the beginnings of quality programs for children in the 1960s and 1970s. General funding was provided through the Corporation for Public Broadcasting, and grants were made to nonprofit producers from the National Science Foundation, the Department of Education, the Bureau for the Education of the Handicapped, and numerous other federal and state agencies. Reductions in government funding of public television and nonprofit producers in the 1980s led to a marked decline in new productions. In 1990 the Congress took a first step toward increasing funding by establishing the National Endowment for Children's Television. Although the initial level of funding is small, it will provide resources for the production of some quality programs.

Adequate numbers of quality children's programs could be funded for a reasonable cost, according to an analysis by Palmer (1988). He proposed an annual children's television schedule containing 780 hours of programming, of which 190 hours per year would be new. Equal numbers of program hours would be targeted to each of three age groups: 2 to 5, 6 to 9, and 10 to 13. The total cost for such programming would be approximately $62 million, or about $1.50 per child in the relevant age groups per year. This proposal is based on the assumption that a cumulative backlog or library of programming could be built over several years—a practice currently used by *Sesame Street* and other highly successful children's programs.

Tax incentives for private corporations have also been proposed as a means of funding programming. Each of these proposals is based on the solid premises that good programming is expensive and that the marketplace forces do not lead to high-quality programming designed to meet children's educational, social, or emotional needs. Some public means of funding are necessary to achieve that goal.

Producing and Disseminating Information
Government agencies play a critical role in creating and disseminating knowledge about mass media and their effects on children and adults. Most of the research described in this book was conducted with government funds. At several points in the short history of television, government agencies have taken the lead in

initiating and organizing research and in producing reports that summarized and integrated available knowledge. Two notable examples are the summary report and five volumes produced by the Surgeon General's Scientific Advisory Committee on Television and Social Behavior (1972; and Comstock & Rubinstein, 1972a; 1972b; Comstock, Rubinstein, & Murray, 1972; Murray, Rubinstein, & Comstock, 1972; Rubinstein, Comstock, & Murray, 1972) and the two volumes produced by the National Institute of Mental Health (1982; Pearl et al., 1982). Although scholarly knowledge is probably not sufficient to direct public policy, it is essential. Without a good foundation of information, both public and private efforts would founder.

Private Advocacy
One of the most effective forces for change in children's programming during the past 20 years has been Action for Children's Television, a citizen-advocate group. It initiates legal actions, proposes and supports legislative efforts, distributes information for parents and other private citizens, and is tireless in fighting to reduce advertising and increase the quality of children's programs. Other citizen-advocate groups concentrate on television violence, morality, or other types of content, and some of them monitor television content. The civil rights movement and the women's movement were both accompanied by major campaigns to change the images of each group in the media; in each case, some successes occurred.

Professional organizations of physicians, psychologists, educators, and others concerned with children have also taken public stands on such issues as television violence. For example, the American Psychological Association (1985) publicly concluded that television violence can cause aggressive behavior and urged broadcasters to reduce violence. Professional organizations also attempt to promote good programming with awards and endorsements. For example, the National Education Association and the PTA identify general-audience programs with educational value. All of these efforts by citizens and professionals may be important, but it is difficult to determine their effects.

Recommended Policy Directions

The public and private efforts to improve television for children and other groups are hampered in the United States by powerful industry opposition and the absence of policies to balance the needs and interests of different constituencies. Of the various policy options discussed, three seem promising within the present social and political context of the United States.

First, it would be useful to return to enforcing the provision of the Communications Act of 1934 that broadcasters must serve the public interest, convenience, and necessity. This provision has been applied most actively to programming for children, but it could well be applied to other populations, including the elderly, ethnic minorities, or women. Regulation can be most effective if it promotes positive steps to meet the needs of different groups in our society. Proposals to require a minimum of informative programming for children are more feasible and consistent with American political values than proposals to prohibit certain types of content. Stations could also be required to demonstrate at the time of license renewal that they were serving the needs of different population groups.

Second, the recent deregulation of program content and advertising has been associated with increased advertising to children. Children are especially vulnerable to sophisticated media advertising appeals. One goal of public policy should be to reduce advertising directed to children in order to protect them from unfair sources of persuasion. A minimum initial move toward this goal has been taken by reinstating limits on the amount of nonprogram material shown in children's television. The next step is to limit or eliminate product-related programs. They not only exploit children's vulnerability, but exclude other programs from broadcast outlets because they are usually subsidized by toy companies, making competition by a nonsubsidized program almost impossible.

Third, quality programming for children requires noncommercial sources of funding. Given the link between profit and programming, one way in which children's television could be improved would be the removal of the economic pressures on programming in this sensitive area. By removing the requirement that each and every program pay its way through advertising, broadcasters would be able to provide specialized programming for small but important audiences. The encapsulation of the economic pressures on broadcasting in this area would have a liberating effect on the structure of children's television.

Just how this improvement of television for children and other minorities should be accomplished has been the subject of considerable debate. One means is to increase support for public television. It has a mandate to meet the needs of groups in society for information and entertainment. Stronger government support for public-television production and distribution as well as mechanisms to raise private funds for noncommercial television are needed. Whatever the means, the critical point is that commercial funding is ill-suited to the task of fostering the social and emotional development of young viewers or the needs of other demographic groups with little economic power. The prospect of a "new season" is not bright unless and until some profound modifications are undertaken that would remove the economic constraints of the mass market from some domains of television.

Although the old problems of broadcast television are still very much in evidence, the new technologies present additional policy issues. Cable and videotapes contain more violent and sexual content than broadcast television, and they are almost entirely dependent on private profit-oriented sources of funding. Cable is minimally subject to regulation by the Federal Communications Commission and by local governments that grant franchises, but there is very little leverage from those sources. Videotapes are not subject to any government controls except local ordinances concerning pornography. However, public funding could be used to promote production and distribution of high-quality programs on both cable and videotape.

SUMMARY

The democratic, developed countries of the world have a wide range of broadcasting systems. Across nations and within countries, programming that is publicly funded is, on the average, more informative and of higher quality than commercially funded programs. Because profits arise from large mass audiences, the marketplace does not support the production and distribution of programs tailored to the needs of demographic and ethnic minorities.

The United States does not have a coherent public policy concerning television, in part because of potential conflicts with freedom of expression. In fact, however, the federal government makes decisions affecting television that might be aided by an articulated policy. Government policy could have two major objectives: (1) promoting quality, diverse programming that serves the needs of all groups of citizens, and (2) protecting citizens from harmful effects. Our review of available programming indicates that neither of these objectives is being reached by current policies and actions.

The Communications Act of 1934 provides that television stations granted licenses must serve the public interest, convenience, and necessity, but most efforts to regulate television in the interests of children or other minority groups have failed. The most promising directions in the 1990s are: requiring a minimum amount of programming designed to suit the needs of particular groups, regulating advertising to children, and generating noncommercial sources of funding for quality programming. The first steps toward these goals with respect to children were taken in 1990 with the passage of new laws that (1) require broadcasters to meet the needs of the child audience, (2) limit the amount of advertising during children's programs, (3) allow broadcasters to cooperate in reducing violence, and (4) establish a National Endowment for Children's Television to fund production of quality programming for children. The advent of new technologies has raised a host of new policy issues. However, the Federal Communications Commission has less jurisdiction over cable distributors than over broadcasters, and it has no regulatory authority regarding videotapes.

Summary and Conclusion

8

Television is woven into the fabric of daily life. The majority of households in the United States have two or more television sets, subscribe to a cable system, and own a videorecorder. One or more of those sets is turned on for several hours a day, and people are watching much of that time. We use television to get information (e.g., to find out about the weather, election results, or new innovations in science), but the most common reason we watch television is to be entertained by comedies, dramas, adventures, game shows, talk shows, and a host of other program genres. However, television is more than mere entertainment. Even when producers and viewers do not intend it as a source of information, it transmits messages about the world and society. People's world views are shaped by a gradual, cumulative process of multiple exposures to frequent messages. The influences of televised messages depend, of course, on the viewer as well as what is broadcast. What people watch and what they glean from what they watch varies with their interests, knowledge, intellectual abilities, and personality attributes.

Three themes guide our consideration of television in the society of the 1990s. First, we are interested in the role of television in the lives of vulnerable or relatively powerless groups in American society—children, the elderly, ethnic minorities, and women. Second, we have gone beyond research about violence to probe less frequently studied issues, such as social relationships, emotion, sexuality, academic skills, and physical and mental health. Third, we are neither pro- nor antitelevision; instead, both the positive and negative contributions of television to modern life are considered.

TELEVISION AND VULNERABLE GROUPS

Children, the elderly, ethnic minorities, and women have in common a position in society that is relatively vulnerable, powerless, low in status, or peripheral. They are more often poorer than their counterparts, white men. They have few representatives in the bastions of political and economic power (e.g., elected political office and high-level corporate executive positions). The low social and economic status of these groups makes them a relatively unattractive audience (or market) for a profit-oriented television industry. It is not surprising, therefore, that most current television programming is not tailored to their needs.

Many of the poorest and most vulnerable groups in our society are also the heaviest users of television, in part because television is a default option used when other activities are not available. The more time people spend at home or near a television set, the more time they are likely to spend viewing. Children, the elderly, institutionalized populations, and many women have limited mobility, so they are apt to watch television more than people who have the physical and financial resources to spend time away from home (or the place in which they live). The ethnic minorities considered in this report are blacks, Hispanics, Asian-Americans, and Native Americans. Large numbers of people belonging to these groups are poor, and they live in urban or rural areas with relatively few opportunities for recreation or leisure away from home. Therefore, they have relatively few alternative forms of entertainment.

Television can serve many special needs. Children benefit from age-specific programs designed to foster their social and intellectual development. On the average, elderly people prefer informational programs and are less interested than younger people in much of the current prime-time drama and entertainment fare. Black Americans especially enjoy entertainment programs with black characters and actors, but we know relatively little about the functions of television for other ethnic groups. Programs in Spanish, Chinese, and other languages are viewed by ethnic minorities who speak those languages, but programs in English may also help immigrants to learn English. Women watch more daytime television than men, but it is not clear whether the reason is program content or simply that women are home. Available programming for children is viewed and preferred by boys more than girls. The needs of girls and women might be better served by more programming portraying females in varied and important roles. Finally, people in institutions could benefit from a variety of programs promoting mental health and prosocial behavior.

The current system of programming serves some of the needs of these subgroups some of the time, but these groups are not usually the high-priority market for most commercial television. Although they are profitable markets for television advertising, they have less disposable income than white male nonelderly adults, so programming designed for them is done cheaply and is often relegated to time periods when more affluent viewers are not readily available (e.g., the Saturday morning children's "ghetto"). Cable systems have expanded offerings for demographic and ethnic minorities because multiple channels permit narrowcasting. Public television serves a variety of information needs of children and adults in many subgroups. Nevertheless, the majority of the viewing audience still tunes to commercial broadcast television; more efforts are needed to induce commercial broadcasters to provide programming suited to the needs of these demographic and ethnic minority groups.

More research is also needed to understand those needs. We know a great deal about the functions of television for children, a modest amount about those for the elderly and women, and relatively little about those for many ethnic minorities or institutionalized populations. More knowledge about television's contributions to physical and mental health for elderly and institutionalized populations could be quite useful. What is known about television and ethnic minorities is limited almost entirely to black Americans. Research on other ethnic groups could be useful to investigate television as a source of language acquisition and acculturation, just to name two examples.

Television Images of Social Groups

Television can reflect and affect the position of groups in the society by its treatment of them. The number and types of portrayals of a group symbolize their importance, power, and social value. Analysts of television content point out that devaluation and stereotyping of social groups can occur in two ways—by excluding them entirely from programs or by presenting negative images when they are portrayed. Each of the groups of concern here is underrepresented on television relative to their numbers in the population. For most, television also conveys negative stereotypes. Women and elderly people are often portrayed as weak, inadequate, and incompetent. There have been recent changes toward less stereotyped portrayals of women, but because television tends to follow social change, we cannot confidently project that these trends will continue. Changes have also occurred in portrayals of gays and lesbians—from nonexistent to moderately sympathetic images.

Women are not only underrepresented in general, but are especially likely to be absent from the screen when they belong to any of the other subgroups of interest. Female characters are especially scarce on children's programs; elderly women are rare; black, Hispanic, Asian, and Native American women are much less frequently shown than men in those groups; and lesbians are shown much less often than gay men.

Most ethnic minorities are virtually absent from the television screen or clustered in a few programs. When they do appear, they are often negatively stereotyped as criminals, dangerous characters, or victims of violence. Blacks appear more often than the other minority groups of interest here, and there have been significant changes in such portrayals in the last 25 years. Blacks now appear in major roles and many are successful television personalities. As in the case of women, however, the change is not linear. In the 1970s, there was an increase in representation, followed by a decrease in the 1980s.

Television portrayals can have two important effects: they may influence the self-images of the subgroups who are (or are not) shown, and they may cultivate attitudes and beliefs about minorities among the wider population. Images of status inequality can both create and maintain inequality in the broader society. The less real-world information viewers have about a social group, the more apt they are to accept the television image of that group. Television appears to cultivate beliefs through a process of gradual accretion when images are repeated often (the drip hypothesis).

Single programs or series may, however, have a strong effect when they are salient (the drench hypothesis). Programs designed to counteract sex stereotypes, for instance, can change children's attitudes and beliefs about what women and men should do. A program like *Golden Girls* may produce changes in stereotypes about older women, as *The Cosby Show* is widely believed to have done for images of black Americans.

Despite the strong theoretical reasons to expect that television is a source of beliefs and attitudes, little solid evidence exists. Not much is known about the positive and negative effects of television portrayals of minorities and other groups in both programs and advertisements. Research is needed on such questions as: How do television portrayals affect perceptions and attitudes of self and the group? Do they provide a means of community support? How do they affect perceptions and attitudes of majority group members toward themselves as well as toward the minority portrayed?

BEYOND VIOLENCE

Social Relationships
Television is a subtle, continuous source of the rules of life and society from which viewers can learn about social relationships, intimacy, conflict, and feeling. Family relations, sexuality, emotion, and violence are the stuff of entertainment television.

Families are central to many of the most popular programs on television. The family types portrayed have shifted over time, only partly reflecting changes in family structure in the society. However, we know relatively little about how television family members interact, what types of parenting are displayed, or what images of children and adolescents are presented. Children and parents alike may use television as a source of norms for family interaction. Families may feel inadequate when comparing themselves to the competent, affluent, and successful families that predominate in prime-time programs. Other program genres, such as cartoons and soap operas, often present models of unhealthy and incompetent family interactions.

We also know remarkably little about the nature of emotions displayed by television characters or about viewers' positive and negative emotional responses to television portrayals. People often seek emotional arousal (if they are bored) or reduction of arousal (if they are under stress) when they watch television. Of course, people's reactions to an emotional portrayal differ. Young children, for example, are frightened by physical changes in characters and monsters; older children react to the fears expressed by characters. People sometimes respond more intensely to events that are real than to those they know are fictional. Emotion is central to the television-viewing process and deserves considerably more systematic study.

Sex on television and in other media (e.g., popular songs) has become a major target of critics. Sexuality is generally suggested rather than shown on broadcast television, but there has been a steady increase in verbal references to sexuality and in sexually suggestive behavior in the last several years. On cable television and videotapes, explicit—and sometimes violent—sex is commonplace.

Television can be a source of sexual learning for children and adolescents, especially when parents and schools fail to provide sex information and education. Children learn a vocabulary about sex from sexually suggestive material, but current evidence does not show that this material influences sexual behavior. Almost all studies of sexually explicit material have been conducted with college students. Exposure to erotic content does not appear to induce antisocial behavior, but watching sexual violence or violence in a sexual context leads to increased acceptance of rape and other forms of sexual violence and instigates antisocial values and behavior.

The bulk of research on television and social behavior has been devoted to violence. American television has been violent for many years. Over the past 20 years, the rate of violence on prime-time evening television has remained at about 5 to 6 incidents per hour, whereas the rate on children's Saturday morning programs is typically 20 to 25 acts per hour. There is clear evidence that television violence can cause aggressive behavior and can cultivate values favoring the use of aggression to resolve conflicts.

Educational Uses

Television is a wonderfully attractive and effective means of supplying knowledge, encouraging language skills, teaching cognitive skills, and instilling prosocial behavior. The evidence shows consistently that planned programs for young children achieve these goals. Most educational and informational programs for children are available on noncommercial television, but funding and production for public television was seriously reduced in the 1980s, resulting in a decline of new productions for children.

Health

Television carries a wealth of messages about physical and mental health—both planned and unplanned. On the one hand, entertainment programs and advertisements show patterns of eating, drinking, and legal drug use that often contradict good health practices. People drink a lot of alcohol on television. They eat rich, calorie-dense foods and remain slim and physically fit. Advertisements to children are permeated with sugar-laden cereals, candy, fat-saturated chips, and fast foods.

There is some evidence that heavy television viewing leads to obesity, but the reasons for the association are not clear. Frequent viewers may act on the nutrition messages they see, or they may simply be less active and more apt to snack while viewing.

Television is also filled with portrayals of medical procedures and illness, but little is known about how these affect viewers' expectations and behavior when they come into contact with medical institutions. We need research to investigate how television portrayals affect health-related behavior (e.g., risky behavior by adolescents). We also need more information about the relation of television to mental health, with an emphasis on possible positive contributions. For example, how do television portrayals of emotion and interpersonal relations influence viewers' feelings and behavior? How do portrayals of emotionally disturbed behavior affect attitudes? How do portrayals of mental-health professionals affect viewer attitudes? How does a heavy diet of television affect people who are institutionalized for mental illness? How does television influence people's fears and anxieties?

Television can be used effectively for promoting good health. Public-service campaigns to encourage diets that are healthy for the heart or to assuage fears during community crises are often effective, particularly in reaching people without high levels of education. Messages about good nutrition can produce attitude change and short-term behavior change (e.g., choosing nutritious food immediately following viewing, or sending food to refugees), but we need much more information about what makes such campaigns effective or ineffective. Moreover, the messages in entertainment programs can quickly counteract the effects of health-oriented public-service announcements.

More research on the impact of public-service persuasion is needed. For example, extensive campaigns are currently underway to combat drug use, but there is little information about whether they are effective or, more importantly, what variables contribute to effectiveness. In all likelihood, effectiveness varies with populations, so such research would require examination of population variables along with media variables. Similar questions arise concerning campaigns to prevent AIDS and other sexually transmitted diseases.

Advertising

Advertising is at the core of American television. There is little doubt that it is effective in persuading viewers of all ages to purchase products. Most social concern about advertising has been devoted to children because they are especially vulnerable to advertising appeals. Young children do not fully understand the purposes of advertising, and they have difficulty distinguishing advertising from programs. They accept commercials uncritically and they ask for and consume advertised products. Children's desire for expensive products can lead to parent-child conflict and the child's disappointment with the types of toys and foods the parent provides.

During the 1970s, guidelines for advertisements to young children were developed by the Federal Communications Commission, and limits on the amount of time devoted to nonprogram material were established. With federal deregulation in the early 1980s, however, the amounts and types of advertising to children increased. In 1990, Congressional legislation reestablished some limits on time devoted to advertisements to children.

Advertising to children is problematic in part because the commercial purpose of broadcasting permeates decisions about program content as well as the content of the advertisements. Advertisers' demands for large, heterogeneous audiences lead them to aim at an audience from 2 through 12 years and prevent the development of age-specific, special programs for smaller groups of viewers. In the 1980s, children's programs became direct marketing vehicles for toys—a phenomenon known as product-related programming. Most of the new programs on commercial television were designed as part of a marketing campaign to feature toys and accessories. Decisions about program content were therefore guided by marketing considerations, not by judgments about what would be most beneficial or even most entertaining to children. As a result, the diversity of children's programs on commercial channels decreased.

In the 1970s, extensive research on children's responses to advertising was conducted, in part because of policy concerns. When the federal government's inclination to regulate dried up in the 1980s, so did research on advertising effects. We need new research that goes beyond what young children understand about advertisements to such questions as: Does heavy viewing of commercial television lead to increased materialism? How does repeated interruption of programs affect attention patterns? Does understanding the purposes of advertising reduce a child's vulnerability to persuasion? Do the effects of advertising vary with the age, gender, or ethnic group of the viewer? Does the consumer pressure generated by advertisements affect family relationships?

Research is also needed on the effects of product-related programming, particularly in light of new legislation instructing the FCC to investigate this issue. Do children recognize the persuasive intent of these programs? Do such programs generate pressures to buy the toys portrayed? How do children respond when their parents cannot or will not purchase the toy? If the toy is needed for interacting with the program, how do children respond with and without it?

Social Issues
Television productions often dramatize such sensitive social issues as suicide or spouse abuse. In many instances, the presentations are serious dramas designed in part to provoke thought and increase awareness of social problems. But these same dramas can have paradoxical effects on a small minority of viewers. They may raise awareness of social problems, but they may also instigate dangerous behavior (e.g., suicide attempts) by susceptible individuals. The solution to this paradox is not clear. Because television is a mass medium, what it offers can be viewed by the whole range of ages and personalities. In the case of suicide, however, programs can be accompanied by information about suicide hotlines and prevention centers that may reach susceptible individuals or people who know them.

TELEVISION — GOOD AND BAD

Social critics and the general public have blamed television for every social ill from declining academic performance to juvenile delinquency. Concentrating on the negatives, however, sometimes leads people to ignore the equally important questions about the positive contributions television does make or could make. Clearly, the content of television can be beneficial or harmful

(Murray & Salomon, 1984). What about the medium of television itself?

Some contend that television as a medium engenders intellectual passivity, displaces creative and intellectually demanding activities, and interferes with school work. The evidence does not support the worst fears of television's critics. Television displaces some activities, but primarily those that are functionally similar to it. Television viewing is associated with low school achievement and low reading ability, but these effects appear to be due to or confounded by low levels of intellectual ability among heavy viewers. On the positive side, properly designed television can teach reading skills and motivate children to read.

Television does not inherently encourage passivity, intellectual or physical. People can watch television actively or passively. Young children's patterns of attention and learning from television demonstrate clearly that when they are absorbed in television they are mentally active and selective. They think about and evaluate what they are seeing. However, the predominance of "pure entertainment" on American television eventually leads viewers to adopt an attitude that television requires little mental effort because they believe the medium is undemanding and are confirmed in this view by the banal nature of many programs.

Television formats, forms, and production techniques can be used to stimulate viewers to think actively about what they are viewing or to interact with the program. Children learn to "read" the production cues denoting interesting and comprehensible content. Well-placed special effects can direct attention, formats can signal important content, and production features can emphasize content messages. These techniques are used in good educational programs to maximize viewer involvement.

Family and School
The effects of television depend not only on the content, but on the viewer. Television content is selected, used, and interpreted by each viewer. Therefore, some of the negative effects may be reduced and some of the positive effects enhanced by interventions that influence program selection and interpretation. Such inter-

ventions have been systematically studied within the family and in school curricula.

Family Influences

Parents are extremely important models for children's viewing habits. Children form stable patterns of viewing early in life, largely on the basis of how parents and siblings use television. Parents can enhance the positive effects of television and moderate some of the negative effects of television by viewing, discussing, and evaluating programs with their children. However, the fact that parents can and should guide their children's viewing does not relieve the television industry and public policymakers from their responsibility to ensure that television offerings are diverse and free from clearly harmful content.

Schools

School curricula that teach media literacy or critical-viewing skills can also be successful in teaching children about television production and advertising. Such curricula help children to understand television and to be skeptical about advertising, but we need considerably more information about how to make them effective influences on children's viewing behavior.

New Technologies

Over a period of many years, cable systems have reached more and more homes and they have expanded the number of channels available, including many for specialized audiences. In the 1980s, home videorecorders spread throughout the country with remarkable speed. These changes open the way for television to serve the needs of a heterogeneous population by increasing the number of outlets and the opportunities for viewers to select programs and control the time and circumstances of viewing. They allow for programming that is diverse and is targeted to specialized audiences (e.g., children, Spanish-speaking minorities). Thus far, cable systems have been more successful than producers of videocassettes in increasing the diversity of programs, but the potential of cassettes is enormous.

Videorecorders and remote controls have the potential to alter the process of viewing. With remote controls, viewers change channels often and sometimes watch two or three programs simultaneously. They switch off the sound and listen to the radio or records while watching the television. Videorecorders and cassettes provide opportunities for active viewing. They allow viewers flexibility of scheduling, the opportunity to control the pace of viewing, and opportunities to repeat or skip segments. Their scheduling flexibility makes in-class educational television much more appealing than broadcast television to many educators. Early research suggests, however, that viewers do not take advantage of the opportunities for reviewing, skipping segments, or interrupting the program for discussion. We need research to track how and whether viewers come to take advantage of these technologies. How does viewing and information processing change with remote controls that allow frequent channel switching? Do people learn more as a result of the opportunities provided by videotapes? How can interactive television be used effectively for learning? Could interactive technology be used for social and emotional learning as well as cognitive learning? How could new technologies be used to improve the value of television to such populations as the elderly or institutionalized individuals?

With the advantages of technological change come some dangers. If we rely on cable and videocassettes to supply diversity and quality in programming, we have imperiled social equity by widening the information and communication gap between the rich and the poor.[7] Moreover, both cable and videotapes contain much more explicit and potentially dangerous sex and violence than broadcast television. Children and adolescents have ready access to such programming, and they watch it. These outlets are not subject to the same legal requirements for serving the public interest that apply to broadcast television and are therefore much more difficult to regulate.

A POLICY FOR TELEVISION?

The United States is almost alone in the world in having no coherent policy about television. One reason is the strong tradition prohibiting government interference with speech. Another is historical. Despite the legal requirement that television should serve the public interest, television developed in this country almost entirely as a commercial medium rather than as a public service. From its beginning, it adopted the model of broadcasting as a profit-making enterprise that was already established for radio.

This commercial organization of broadcasting is the most fundamental determinant of program content. When broadcasting relies primarily on advertiser support, programming decisions are based largely on anticipated profits. The principal goal is to attract the largest possible audience of viewers who fall in high income demographic categories and can buy expensive products. The target audience for many prime-time programs, for example, is adults between 18 and 49 with large disposable incomes. Many of the groups of concern in this book receive relatively little attention from commercial broadcasters because they are not lucrative markets for advertising.

Public television was established in the United States to meet viewers' needs for informative programming, and its programming fulfills that mission. However, the funding base for public television is inadequate, and it was reduced considerably in the 1980s. Public television stations now rely heavily on viewer contributions, a funding source that is unstable and insufficient.

The association between revenue source and program content is not peculiar to the United States. Across nations, broadcasting systems in which revenues are derived principally from advertising tend to be oriented primarily to entertainment programming. Cross-national comparisons show that systems based on noncommercial funding are apt to contain diverse programming, including informative programs and high-quality entertainment. More current and systematic cross-national investigations could provide useful comparative information to determine means of stimulating quality programming. Even though it would not be reasonable to import another country's broadcasting system, the United States could gain new ideas about how to provide diverse, high-quality programming.

The United States should have a television policy. The federal government makes decisions affecting television almost daily, and it is only reasonable that such decisions should be based on an articulated set of principles. At its most fundamental level, government policy should have two objectives: (1) promoting quality, diverse programming that serves needs of all groups of citizens, and (2) protecting citizens and society from harmful effects. Our review of available programming indicates that neither of these objectives is being reached by current policies and actions.

A more effective policy could be enacted by enforcing the provisions of the Communications Act of 1934 that broadcasters must serve the public interest, convenience, and necessity. In recent years, this provision has been cited in arguments about programming for children, but it could be applied as well to other populations, such as the elderly, ethnic minorities, or women. Recently enacted legislation to require broadcasters to meet the educational and informational needs of children is an example of a positive step to generate diverse programming. Limits on the amount of advertising and steps to curtail product-based programs enacted into law in 1990 are important to protect children from excessive merchandising. Product-based programs are not only advertising in disguise, but they exclude other programs from broadcast outlets because they are usually subsidized by toy companies, making competition by a nonsubsidized program almost impossible.

The most important change needed in our broadcasting system, however, is to increase noncommercial sources of funding. So long as the primary goal of programming is to lure audiences to advertisements, the needs of many demographic and ethnic minorities will not be met. One means of accomplishing this goal is to increase support for public television. It has a mandate to meet minority groups' needs for information and entertainment which it is fulfilling. The National Endowment for Children's Television, established by Congress in 1990, is a first step in providing funding for children's programming, but more is needed. A second means of increasing relevant programming is to find ways to ensure cable access for all citizens. Cable produces diverse programs, but raises serious issues of information equity because of its cost to subscribers. A third is to promote production and distribution of high-quality educational and informational videotapes, incorporating efforts to provide access by a wide range of individuals through libraries, schools, and other means. Finally, the potentials of interactive television have only been glimpsed thus far, despite the fact that the technology has been available for some time. Apparently, interactive television is not yet profitable; it is an ideal domain in which nonprofit educational innovations can occur.

Public policy for television cannot occur in a societal vacuum. Private citizens, advocates, professional organizations, and political organizations must complement, support, and reinforce public policy if it is to be effective. Such groups can monitor television content, offer public evaluations of programs, and help to provide funding. Positive and negative commentary about commercial television can be effective if there are implications for profits. For example, networks are quite receptive to information about program appeal. It is helpful to use successful programs such as *The Cosby Show* as examples of principles being advocated.

POSTSCRIPT

We end this book with a few answers and many challenges. Television is an all-important feature of modern life and, at the same time, an elusive target of study. One reason is that "television" is constantly changing, and the ways that people use it change, too. In 40 years, we have gone from a small black-and-white set with a few programs watched eagerly by family and neighborhood groups, to multiple sets with color, cable systems with 30 to 100 channels, videorecorders, and wall-sized screens. The total viewing time for adults increased when broadcasters discovered a morning adult audience, and scheduling flexibility became the rule. All of these changes have been unplanned, in the sense that public policy did little to affect them or to adapt to them. We in this country have let television follow its commercial course with little effort to use it for purposes other than entertainment.

Our failure to realize the potential benefits of the medium is perhaps more significant than our inability to control some of its harmful effects. For several years, the nation's educational crisis has been bewailed by educators and government officials. Other countries use television to educate their children from the preschool years on. We in the United States could use some of the hours that children spend in front of the set to stimulate their minds, stretch their horizens, and teach them about the world. For some of the time that elderly people, minorities, and women spend watching television we could provide programming that meets their needs for information, group identity, and knowledge about the diverse society in which we live. Whether we *will* do so is the central question that remains.

References

Adams, M., & Groen, R. (1974). *Reaching the retired: A survey of the media habits, preferences, and needs of senior citizens in Metro Toronto.* Ottawa, Canada: Information Canada (Catalog No. BC 92-9/1974).

Adler, R. P., & Faber, R. J. (1980). Background: Children's television viewing patterns. In R. P. Adler, G. S. Lesser, L. K. Meringoff, T. S. Robertson, J. R. Rossiter, & S. Ward, *The effects of television advertising on children.* Lexington, MA: Lexington Books.

Altman, D. (1982). *The homosexualization of America: The Americanization of homosexuals.* New York: St. Martin's Press.

Alvarez, M., Huston, A. C., Wright, J. C., & Kerkman, D. (1988). Gender differences in visual attention to television form and content. *Journal of Applied Developmental Psychology, 9,* 459-476.

Alwitt, L. F., Anderson, D. R., Lorch, E. P., & Levin, S. R. (1980). Preschool children's visual attention to attributes of television. *Human Communication Research, 7,* 52-67.

Alwitt, L. F., & Mitchell, A. (1985). *Psychological processes and advertising effects: Theory, research, and applications.* Hillsdale, NJ: Erlbaum.

American Institute for Public Opinion Research. (1987, March 23). *Newsletter,* p.3.

American Psychological Association (1985). *Violence on television.* Washington, DC: APA Board of Social and Ethical Responsibility for Psychology.

Anderson, D. R., & Collins, P. A. (1988). *The impact on children's education: Television's influence on cognitive development.* Washington, DC: U.S. Department of Education.

Anderson, D. R., & Field, D. E. (1983). Children's attention to television: Implications for production. In M. Meyer (Ed.), *Children and the formal features of television* (pp.56–96). München: K. G. Saur.

Anderson, D. R., Levin, S. R., & Lorch, E. P. (1977). The effects of TV program pacing on the behavior of preschool children. *AV Communication Review, 25,* 154–166.

Anderson, D. R., & Lorch, E. P. (1983). Looking at television: Action or reaction? In J. Bryant & Dr. R. Anderson (Eds.), *Children's understanding of television: Research on attention and comprehension* (pp.1–33). New York: Academic Press.

Anderson, D. R., Lorch, E. P., Field, D. E., Collins, P. A., & Nathan, J. G. (1986). Television viewing at home: Age trends in visual attention and time with TV. *Child Development, 57,* 1024–1033.

Atkin, C. (1975a). *Effects of television advertising on children: First year experimental evidence* (Tech. Rep. No. 1). East Lansing: Michigan State University.

Atkin, C. (1975b). *Effects of television advertising on children: Survey of preadolescents' responses to television commercials* (Tech. Rep. No. 6). East Lansing: Michigan State University.

Atkin, C. (1978). Observation of parent-child interaction in supermarket decision making. *Journal of Marketing, 42,* 41–45.

Atkin, C., & Block, M. (1983). Effectiveness of celebrity endorsers. *Journal of Advertising Research, 23*(1), 57–61.

Atkin, C., & Heald, G. (1977). The content of children's toy and food commercials. *Journal of Communication, 27*(1), 107–114.

Atkin, C. K. (1982). Television advertising and socialization to consumer roles. In D. Pearl, L. Bouthilet, & J. Lazar (Eds.), *Television and behavior: Ten years of scientific progress and implications for the eighties* (vol.2), *Technical reviews* (pp.191–200). Washington, DC: U.S. Government Printing Office.

Baker, R. K., & Ball, S. J. (1969). *Violence and the media: A report to the national Commission on the Causes and Prevention of Violence.* Washington, DC: U.S. Government Printing Office.

Ball, S., & Bogatz, G. A. (1970). *The first year of Sesame Street: An evaluation.* Princeton, NJ: Educational Testing Service.

Ball, S., & Bogatz, G. A. (1973). *Reading with television: An evaluation of "The Electric Company"* (2 vols.). Princeton, NJ: Educational Testing Service.

Ballard-Campbell, M. (1983). *Children's understanding of television advertising: Behavioral assessment of three developmental skills.* Unpublished doctoral dissertation, University of California, Los Angeles.

Bandura, A. (1977). *Social learning theory.* Englewood Cliffs, NJ: Prentice-Hall.

Bandura, A., & Menlove, F. L. (1968). Factors determining vicarious extinction of avoidance behavior through symbolic modeling. *Journal of Personality and Social Psychology, 8,* 99–108.

Bandura, A., Ross, D., & Ross, S. (1961). Transmission of aggression through imitation of aggressive models. *Journal of Abnormal and Social Psychology, 63,* 575–582.

Bandura, A., Ross, D., & Ross, S. (1963). Imitation of film-mediated aggressive models. *Journal of Abnormal and Social Psychology, 66,* 3–11.

Bantz, C. R. (1982). Exploring uses and gratifications. A comparison of reported uses of television and reported uses of favorite program type. *Communication Research, 9,* 352–379.

Barcus, F. E. (1977). *Children's television: An analysis of programming and advertising.* New York: Praeger.

Barcus, F. E. (1980). The nature of television advertising to children. In E. L. Palmer & A. Dorr (Eds.), *Children and the faces of television: Teaching, violence, selling* (pp.273–286). New York: Academic Press.

Barcus, F. E. (1983). *Images of life on children's television: Sex roles, minorities, and families.* New York: Praeger.

Barry, T., & Sheikh, A. (1977). Race as a dimension in children's television advertising: The need for more research. *Journal of Advertising, 6,* 5–10.

Barry, T. E., & Hansen, R. W. (1973). How race affects children's TV commercials. *Journal of Advertising Research, 13*(5), 63–67.

Barton, R. L. (1977). Soap operas provide meaningful communication for the elderly. *Feedback* (Broadcast Education Association), *19,* 5–8.

Bayles, M. (1985). Blacks on TV: Adjusting the image. *New Perspectives, 17*(3), 2–6.

Bearden, W., Teel, J., & Wright, R. (1979). Family income effects on measurement of children's attitudes toward television commercials. *Journal of Consumer Research, 6,* 308–311.

Bechtel, R. B., Achelpohl, C., & Akers, R. (1972). Correlates between observed behavior and questionnaire responses on television viewing.

In E. A. Rubinstein, G. A. Comstock, & J. P. Murray (Eds.), *Television and social behavior* (vol.4), *Television in day-to-day life: Patterns of use* (pp.274–344). Washington, DC: U.S. Government Printing Office.

Belson, W. A. (1967). *The impact of television.* London: Cheshire Publishers.

Belson, W. A. (1978). *Television violence and the adolescent boy.* Farnborough, Hampshire, England: Saxon House, Teakfield Limited.

Berkowitz, L. (1962). *Aggression: A social psychological analysis.* New York: McGraw-Hill.

Berkowitz, L. (1984). Some effects of thoughts on anti- and prosocial influences of media events: A cognitive-neoassociation analysis. *Psychological Bulletin, 95,* 410–427.

Berkowitz, L., Corwin, R., & Heironimus, M. (1963). Film violence and subsequent aggressive tendencies. *Public Opinion Quarterly, 27,* 217–229.

Berkowitz, L., & Rawlings, F. (1963). Effects of film violence on inhibitions against subsequent aggression. *Journal of Abnormal and Social Psychology, 66,* 405–412.

Berkowitz, L., and Rogers, K. H. (1986). A priming effect analysis of media influences. In J. Bryant & D. Zillman (Eds.), *Perspectives on media effects* (pp.57–82). Hillsdale, NJ: Erlbaum.

Berry, G., & Mitchell-Kernan, C. (Eds.). (1982). *Television and the socialization of the minority child.* New York: Academic Press.

Berry, G. L. (1980). Television and Afro-Americans: Past legacy and present portrayals. In S. B. Withey & R. P. Abeles (Eds.), *Television and social behavior: Beyond violence toward children.* Hillsdale, NJ: Erlbaum.

Berry, G. L. (1988). Multicultural role portrayals on television as a social psychological issue. In S. Oskamp (Ed.), *Applied social psychology annual* (vol.8), *Television as a social issue* (pp.118–129). Newbury Park, CA: Sage.

Blatt, J., Spencer, L., & Ward, S. (1972). A cognitive developmental study of children's reactions to television advertising. In E. A. Rubinstein, G. A. Comstock, & J. Murray (Eds.), *Television and social behavior* (vol.4), *Television in day-to-day life: Patterns of use* (pp.452–467). Washington, DC: U.S. Government Printing Office.

Blumler, J. G., & Katz, E. (Eds.). (1974). *The uses of mass communications: Current perspectives on gratifications research.* Beverly Hills, CA: Sage.

Bogatz, G. A., & Ball, S. (1971). *The second year of "Sesame Street": A continuing evaluation* (2 vols.). Princeton, NJ: Educational Testing Service.

Bollen, K. A., & Phillips, D. P. (1982). Imitative suicides: A national study of the effects of television news stories. *American Sociological Review, 47,* 802–809.

Bower, R. T. (1973). *Television and the Public.* New York: Holt, Rinehart & Winston.

Brown, L. K. (1986). *Taking advantage of media: A manual for parents and teachers.* Boston: Routledge & Kegan Paul.

Brown, T. (1982, October 14). How to watch white TV. *Sun Reporter,* p.6.

Bryant, J. (Ed.). (1990). *Television and the American Family.* Hillsdale, NJ: Erlbaum.

Bryant, J., & Anderson, D. R. (Eds.). (1983). *Children's understanding of television: Research on attention and comprehension.* New York: Academic Press.

Bryant, J., & Zillmann, D. (1977). The mediating effect of the intervention potential of communications on displaced aggressiveness and retaliatory behavior. In B. D. Ruben (Ed.), *Communication Yearbook 1.* New Brunswick, NJ: ICA-Transaction Press.

Bryant, J., & Zillmann, D. (1984). Using television to alleviate boredom and stress: Selective exposure as a function of induced excitational states. *Journal of Broadcasting, 28,* 1–20.

Bryant, J., Zillmann, D., & Brown, D. (1983). Entertainment features in children's educational television: Effects on attention and information acquisition. In J. Bryant & D. R. Anderson (Eds.), *Children's understanding of television: Research on attention and comprehension* (pp.221–240). New York: Academic Press.

Buerkel-Rothfuss, N. L., Greenberg, B. S., Atkin, C. K., & Neuendorf, K. (1982). Learning about the family from television. *Journal of Communication, 32,* 191–200.

Butler, M., & Paisley, W. (1980). *Women and the mass media.* New York: Human Sciences Press.

Butsch, R. J., & Glennon, L. M. (1980). Families on TV: Where was the working class? *Television, 7,* 10–12.

Butter, E. J., Popovitch, P. M., Stackhouse, R. H., & Garner, R. K. (1981). Discrimination of television programs and commercials by preschool children. *Journal of Advertising Research, 21*(2), 53–56.

Calvert, S. L., & Gersh, T. L. (1987). The selective use of sound effects and visual inserts for children's television story comprehension. *Journal of Applied Developmental Psychology, 8,* 363–376.

Calvert, S. L., & Huston, A. C. (1987). Television and children's gender schemata. In L. Liben & M. Signorella (Eds.), *New Directions in Child Development* (vol.38), *Children's gender schemata: Origins and implications* (75–88). San Francisco: Jossey-Bass.

Calvert, S. L., Huston, A. C., Watkins, B. A., & Wright, J. C. (1982). The relation between selective attention to television forms and children's comprehension of content. *Child Development, 53,* 601–610.

Calvert, S. L., Huston, A. C., & Wright, J. C. (1987). Effects of television preplay formats on children's attention and story comprehension. *Journal of Applied Developmental Psychology, 8,* 329–342.

Campbell, T. A., Wright, J. C., & Huston, A. C. (1987). Form cues and content difficulty as determinants of children's cognitive processing of televised educational messages. *Journal of Experimental Child Psychology, 43,* 311–327.

Cantor, J., & Reilly, S. (1982). Adolescents' enduring fright reactions to television and films. *Journal of Communication, 32*(1), 87–99.

Cantor, J., & Sparks, G. G. (1984). Children's fear responses to mass media: Testing some Piagetian predictions. *Journal of Communication, 34*(2), 90–103.

Cantor, J., & Wilson, B. J. (1984). Modifying fear responses to mass media in preschool and elementary school children. *Journal of Broadcasting, 28,* 431–443.

Cantor, J., Wilson, B. J., & Hoffner, C. (1986). Emotional responses to a televised nuclear holocaust film. *Communication Research, 13,* 257–277.

Cantor, J., Ziemke, D., & Sparks, G. G. (1984). Effect of forewarning on emotional responses to a horror film. *Journal of Broadcasting, 28,* 21–31.

Cantor, M. G., & Cantor, J. M. (1984). Do soaps teach sex? *Television and Children, 7,* 34–38.

Caron, A., & Ward, S. (1975). Gift decisions by kids and parents. *Journal of Advertising Research, 15*(4), 15–20.

Carruthers, M., & Taggert, P. (1973). Vagotonicity of violence: Biochemical and cardiac responses to violent films and television programmes. *British Medical Journal, 3,* 384–389.

CBS Broadcast Group (1974). *A study of messages received by children who viewed an episode of "Fat Albert and the Cosby Kids."* New York: Office of Social Research, Department of Economics and Research, CBS Broadcast Group.

Chesebro, J. W. (Ed.). (1981). *Gayspeak.* New York: Pilgrim Press.

Christ, W. G., & Medoff, N. J. (1984). Affective state and the selective exposure to and use of television. *Journal of Broadcasting, 28,* 21–31.

Christenson, P. G. (1982). Children's perceptions of TV commercials and products: The effects of PSAs. *Communications Research, 9,* 491–524.

Clancy-Hepburn, K., Hickey, A. A., & Neville, G. (1974). Children's behavior responses to TV food advertisements. *Journal of Nutrition Education, 6,* 93–96.

Clark, C. (1972). Race, identification, and television violence. In G. A. Comstock, E. A. Rubinstein, & J. P. Murray (Eds.), *Television and social behavior* (vol.5), *Television's effects: Further explorations* (pp.120–184). Washington, DC: U.S. Government Printing Office.

Cline, V. B., Croft, R. G., & Courrier, S. (1973). Desensitization of children to television violence. *Journal of Personality and Social Psychology, 27,* 360–365.

Coates, B., Pusser, H. E., & Goodman, I. (1976). The influence of Sesame Street and Mister Rogers' Neighborhood on children's behavior in the preschool. *Child Development, 47,* 138–144.

Collins, W. A. (1983). Interpretation and inference in children's television viewing. In J. Bryant & D. R. Anderson (Eds.), *Children's understanding of television: Research on attention and comprehension* (pp.125–150). New York: Academic Press.

Collins, W. A., & Getz, S. K. (1976). Children's social responses following modeled reactions to provocation: Prosocial effects of a television drama. *Journal of Personality, 44,* 488–500.

Collins, W. A., Sobol, B. L., & Westby, S. (1981). Effects of adult commentary on children's comprehension and inferences about a televised aggressive portrayal. *Child Development, 49,* 389–399.

Comstock, G. (1980). Television entertainment: Taking it seriously. *Character, 1*(12), 1–8.

Comstock, G., Chaffee, N., Katzman, N., McCombs, M., & Roberts, D. (1978). *Television and human behavior.* New York: Columbia University Press.

Comstock, G., & Cobbey, R. E. (1982). Television and the children of ethnic minorities: Perspectives from research. In G. L. Berry & C. Mitchell-Kernan (Eds.), *Television and the socialization of the minority child* (pp.245-260). New York: Academic Press.

Comstock, G. A., & Rubinstein, E. A. (Eds.). (1972). *Television and social behavior* (vol.1), *Media content and control.* Washington, DC: U.S. Government Printing Office.

Comstock, G. A., & Rubinstein, E. A. (Eds.). (1972). *Television and social behavior* (vol.3), *Television and adolescent aggressiveness.* Washington DC: U.S. Government Printing Office.

Comstock, G. A., Rubinstein, E. A., & Murray, J. P. (Eds.). (1972). *Television and social behavior* (vol.5), *Television's effects: Further explorations.* Washington, DC: U.S. Government Printing Office.

Condry, J. (1989). *The psychology of television.* Hillsdale, NJ: Erlbaum.

Condry, J., Bence, P., & Scheibe, C. (1988). The non-program content of children's television. *Journal of Broadcasting and Electronic Media, 32,* 255-270.

Cook, T. D., Appleton, H., Conner, R. F., Shaffer, A., Tamkin, G., & Weber, S. J. (1975). *"Sesame Street" revisited.* New York: Russell Sage.

Cook, T. D., Kendziersky, D. A., & Thomas, S. V. (1983). The implicit assumptions of television: An analysis of the 1982 NIMH report on television and behavior. *Public Opinion Quarterly, 47,* 161-201.

Corteen, R. S., & Williams, T. M. (1986). Television and reading skills. In T. M. Williams (Ed.), *The impact of television: A natural experiment in three communities* (pp.39-85). Orlando, FL: Academic Press.

Davis, D. M. (in press). Portrayals of women in prime time network television: Some demographic characteristics. *Sex Roles.*

Davis, M. H. (1983). Empathic concern and the muscular dystrophy telethon: Empathy as a multidimensional construct. *Personality and Social Psychology Bulletin, 9,* 223-229.

Davis, M. H., Hull, J. G., Young, R. D., & Warren, G. G. (1987). Emotional reactions to dramatic film stimuli: The influence of cognitive and emotional empathy. *Journal of Personality and Social Psychology, 52,* 126-133.

Davis, R. H. (1971). Television and the older adult. *Journal of Broadcasting, 15,* 153-159.

Davis, R. H. (1975). Television and the image of aging. *Television Quarterly, 12,* 21-24.

Davis, R. H., & Davis, J. A. (1986). *TV's image of the elderly.* Lexington, MA: Lexington Books.

Davis, R. H., & Kubey, R. W. (1982). Growing old on television and with television. In D. Pearl, L. Bouthilet, & J. Lazar (Eds.), *Television and behavior: Ten years of scientific progress and implications for the eighties* (vol.2), *Technical reports* (pp.201–208). Washington, DC: U.S. Department of Health and Human Services.

Deutsch, F. (1974). Female preschoolers' perceptions of affective responses and interpersonal behavior in videotaped episodes. *Developmental Psychology, 10,* 733–740.

Dietz, W. H., & Gortmaker, S. L. (1985). Do we fatten our children at the television set? Obesity and television viewing in children and adolescents. *Pediatrics, 75,* 807–812.

Donnerstein, E., Linz, D., & Penrod, S. (1987). *The question of pornography: Research findings and policy implications.* New York: Free Press.

Donohue, T. R., Henke, L., & Donohue, W. (1980). Do kids know what TV commercials intend? *Journal of Advertising Research, 20*(5), 51–57.

Donohue, T. R., Meyer, T., & Henke, L. (1978). Black and white children: Perceptions of television commercials. *Journal of Marketing, 42*(4), 34–40.

Doolittle, J., & Pepper, R. (1975). Children's TV ad content: 1974. *Journal of Broadcasting, 19*(2), 131–141.

Dorr, A. (1982). Television and affective development and functioning. In D. Pearl, L. Bouthilet, & J. Lazar (Eds.), *Television and behavior: Ten years of scientific progress and implications for the eighties* (vol.2), *Technical reports* (pp.68–77). Rockville, MD: National Institute of Mental Health.

Dorr, A. (1986). *Television and children: A special medium for a special audience.* Beverly Hills, CA: Sage.

Dorr, A., Doubleday, C., & Kovaric, P. (1983). Emotions depicted on and stimulated by television programs. In M. Meyer (Ed.), *Children and the formal features of television* (pp.97–143). Munich: K. G. Saur.

Dorr, A., Doubleday, C., Kovaric, P., & Kunkel, D. (1981). *An evaluation of NBC's 1980-81 prosocial children's programming: Drawing power, play-alongs, how to watch TV.* Report to the National Broadcasting

Company. Los Angeles: University of California, Graduate School of Education. (ERIC Document Reproduction Service No. ED 216 796).

Dorr, A., Graves, S. B., & Phelps, E. (1980). Television literacy for young children. *Journal of Communication, 30*(3), 71–83.

Dorr, A., Kovaric P., & Doubleday, C. (1989). Parent-child coviewing of television. *Journal of Broadcasting and Electronic Media, 33,* 35–51.

Dorr, A., Kovaric, P., & Doubleday, C. (1990). Age and content influences on children's perceptions of the realism of television families. *Journal of Broadcasting and Electronic Media, 34,* 377–397.

Dorr, A., & Kunkel, D. (1990). Children and the media environment: Change and constancy amid change. *Communication Research, 17,* 5–25.

Doubleday, C., Kovaric, P., Dorr, A., & Beizer-Seidner, L. (1986, August). *Children's knowledge of cultural norms for emotional expression and behavior.* Paper presented at the annual meeting of the American psychological Association, Washington, DC.

Drabman, R. S., & Thomas, M. H. (1974). Does media violence increase children's toleration of real-life aggression? *Developmental Psychology, 10,* 418–421.

Durkin, K. (1985a). Television and sex-role acquisition 1: Content. *British Journal of Social Psychology, 24,* 101–113.

Durkin, K. (1985b). Television and sex-role acquisition 2: Effects. *British Journal of Social Psychology, 24,* 191–210.

Durkin, K. (1985c). Television and sex-role acquisition 3: Counterstereotyping. *British Journal of Social Psychology, 24,* 211–222.

Dysinger, W. S., & Ruckmick, C. A. (1933). *The emotional responses of children to the motion picture situation.* New York: MacMillan.

Ekman, P., Liebert, R. M., Friesen, W. V., Harrison, R., Zlatchin, C., Malmstrom, E. J., & Baron, R. (1972). Facial expressions of emotions while watching televised violence as predictors of subsequent aggression. In G. A. Comstock, E. A. Rubinstein, & J. P. Murray (Eds.), *Television and Social Behavior* (vol.5), *Television effects: Further explorations* (pp.22–58). Washington, DC: U.S. Government Printing Office.

Ellis, G. T., & Sekyra, F. (1972). The effect of aggressive cartoons on the behavior of first grade children. *Journal of Psychology, 81,* 37–43.

Eron, L. (1963). Relationship of TV viewing habits and aggressive behavior in children. *Journal of Abnormal and Social Psychology, 67,* 193–196.

Eron, L. D. (1982). Parent child interaction, television violence and aggression of children. *American Psychologist, 27*, 197–211.

Eron, L. D., Lefkowitz, M. M., Huesmann, L. R., & Walder, L. O. (1972). Does television violence cause aggression? *American Psychologist, 27*, 253–263.

Ettema, J. S., Brown, J. W., & Luepker, R. V. (1983). Knowledge gap effects in a health information campaign. *Public Opinion Quarterly, 47*, 516–527.

Eyre-Brook, C. (Ed.). (1972). *Young people and television: An international study of juries, producers, and their audiences based on the prize-winning programmes of the Prix Jeunesse 1970. Man in metropolis and baff*. Munich: Internationales Zentralinstitut fur das Jugend- und Bildungfcrensehen.

Eysenck, H. J., & Nias, D.K.B. (1978). *Sex, violence and the media*. London: Temple Smith.

Fairchild, H. H. (1984). Creating, producing, and evaluating prosocial TV. *Journal of Educational Television, 10*(3), 161–183.

Fairchild, H. H. (1988). Creating positive television images. In S. Oskamp (Ed.), *Applied Social Psychology Annual* (vol.8), *Television as a social issue* (pp.270–279). Newbury Park, CA: Sage.

Federal Communications Commission (1979). Television programming for children: A report of the Children's Television Task Force. Washington, DC: U.S. Government Printing Office.

Federal Trade Commission (1978). FTC *Staff report on television advertising to children*. Washington, DC: U.S. Government Printing Office.

Feldman, S., & Sigelman, L. (1985). The political impact of prime-time television: "The Day After." *Journal of Politics, 47*, 556–578.

Feldstein, J. H., & Feldstein, S. (1982). Sex differences on televised toy commercials. *Sex Roles, 8*, 581–587.

Fcshbach, N. D. (1988). Television and the development of empathy. In S. Oskamp (Ed.), *Applied social psychology annual* (vol.8), *Television as a social issue* (261–269). Newbury Park, CA: Sage.

Feshbach, N. D., Dillman, A. S., & Jordan, T. S. (1979). Portrait of a female on television: Some possible effects on children. In C. B. Kopp (Ed.), *Becoming female: Perspectives on development* (pp.363–385). New York: Plenum Press.

Feshbach, N. D., & Roe, K. (1968). Empathy in six and seven-year-olds. *Child Development, 39*, 133–145.

Feshbach, S., Feshbach, N. D., & Cohen, S. (1983). Enhancing children's discrimination in response to television advertising: The effects of psychoeducational training in two elementary school-aged groups. *Developmental Review, 2,* 385–403.

Feshbach, S., & Singer, R. D. (1971). *Television and aggression: An experimental field study.* New York: Jossey Bass.

Field, D. E. (1989). *Television coviewing related to family characteristics and cognitive performance.* Unpublished doctoral dissertation, University of Massachusetts, Amherst, MA.

Filipson, E., Schyller, I., & Hoijer, B. (1974, July). *Pretesting of the programme "Why Must We Die."* Stockholm, Sweden: Swedish Broadcasting Corporation, Audiences Programme and Research Department.

Fitch, M., Huston, A. C., & Wright, J. C. (1990). *Viewing patterns of adult men and women.* Unpublished manuscript, CRITC, University of Kansas, Lawrence, KS.

Frank, R., & Greenberg, M. (1979). Zooming in on TV audiences. *Psychology Today, 73,* 94–114.

Freedman, J. (1988). The changing composition of the family and the workplace. In E. F. Zigler & M. Frank (Eds.), *The parental leave crisis* (pp.23–35). New Haven, CT: Yale University Press.

Freedman, J. L. (1984). Effect of television violence on aggressiveness. *Psychological Bulletin, 96*(2), 227–246.

Freedman, J. L. (1986). Television violence and aggression: A rejoinder. *Psychological Bulletin, 100,* 372–378.

Friedrich, L. K., & Stein, A. H. (1973). Aggressive and prosocial television programs and the natural behavior of preschool children. *Monographs of the Society for Research in Child Development, 38* (Serial No. 151).

Friedrich, L. K., & Stein, A. H. (1975). Prosocial television and young children's behavior: The effect of verbal labeling and role playing training. *Child Development, 46,* 27–38.

Friedrich-Cofer, L., & Huston, A. C. (1986). Television violence and aggression: The debate continues. *Psychological Bulletin, 100,* 364–371.

Friedrich-Cofer, L., Huston-Stein, A., Kipnis, D. M., Susman, E. J., & Clewett, A. S. (1979). Environmental enhancement of prosocial television content: Effects on interpersonal behavior, imaginative play, and self-regulation in a natural setting. *Developmental Psychology, 15,* 637–646.

Frost, R., & Stauffer, J. (1987). The effects of social class, gender, and personality on physiological responses to filmed violence. *Journal of Communication, 37*(2), 29–45.

Frueh, T., & McGee, P. E. (1975). Traditional sex role development and amount of time spent watching television. *Child Development, 11*, 109.

Gadberry, S. (1974). Television as baby-sitter: A field comparison of preschoolers' behavior during playtime and during television viewing time. *Child Development, 45*, 1132–1136.

Gadberry, S. (1980). Effects of restricting first graders' TV-viewing on leisure time use, IQ change, and cognitive style. *Journal of Applied Developmental Psychology, 1*, 45–58.

Galloway, B. (Ed.). (1983). *Prejudice and pride: Discrimination against gay people in modern Britain.* London: Routledge & Kegan Paul.

Galst, J., & White, M. (1976). The unhealthy persuader: The reinforcing value of television and children's purchase-influencing attempts at the supermarket. *Child Development, 47*, 1089–1096.

Gantz, W. (1985). Exploring the role of television in married life. *Journal of Broadcasting and Electronic Media, 29*, 65–78.

Garfinkel, I., & McLanahan, S. S. (1986). *Single mothers and their children: A new American dilemma.* Washington, DC: The Urban Institutes Press.

Garry, R. (Ed.) (1970). *Findings and cognition on the television perceptions of children and young people based on the prize-winning program of Prix Jeunesse 1968: The Scarecrow.* Munich: Internationales Zentralinstitut fur das Jugend- und Bildungfernsehen.

Geen, R. G. (1975). The meaning of observed violence: Real vs. fictional violence and consequent effects on aggression and emotional arousal. *Journal of Research in Personality, 9*, 270–281.

Geen, R. G., & Rakowsky, J. J. (1973). Interpretations of observed aggression and their effect on GSR. *Journal of Experimental Research in Personality, 6*, 289–292.

Gerbner, G. (1972). Violence in television drama: Trends and symbolic functions. In G. A. Comstock & E. A. Rubinstein (Eds.), *Television and Social Behavior* (vol. 1), *Media Content and Control* (pp. 28–187). Washington, DC: U. S. Government Printing Office.

Gerbner, G. (1980). Symposium on television entertainment: Response. *Character, 2*(1), 2–3.

Gerbner, G., & Gross, L. (1980). The violent face of television and its lessons. In E. L. Palmer & A. Dorr (Eds.), *Children and the faces of television: Teaching, violence, selling* (pp.149–162). New York: Academic Press.

Gerbner, G., Gross, L., Eleey, M. F., Jackson-Beeck, M., Jeffries-Fox, S., & Signorielli, N. (1977). TV violence profile no. 8: The highlights. *Journal of Communication, 27*(2), 171–180.

Gerbner, G., Gross, L., Eleey, M. F., Jackson-Beeck, M., Jeffries-Fox, S., & Signorielli, N. (1978). Cultural indicators: Violence profile no. 9. *Journal of Communication, 28*(3), 176–207.

Gerbner, G., Gross, L., Morgan, M., & Signorielli, N. (1980). The "mainstreaming" of America: Violence profile no. 11. *Journal of Communication, 30*(3), 10–27.

Gerbner, G., Gross, L., Morgan, M., & Signorielli, N. (1986). Living with television: The dynamics of the cultivation process. In J. Bryant & D. Zillmann (Eds.), *Perspectives on media effects* (pp.17–40). Hillsdale, NJ: Erlbaum.

Gerbner, G., Morgan, M., & Signorielli, N. (1982). Programming health portrayals: What viewers see, say and do. In D. Pearl, L. Bouthilet, & J. Lazar (Eds.), *Television and behavior: Ten years of scientific progress and implications for the eighties* (vol.2), *Technical reviews* (pp.291–307). Washington, DC: U.S. Government Printing Office.

Gerbner, G., & Signorielli, N. (1990). *Violence Profile, 1967 through 1988-89: Enduring patterns.* Unpublished manuscript, University of Pennsylvania, Annenberg School of Communications.

Gething, L. (1984). Media and the disabled. *Media Information Australia, 34,* 41–50.

Gist, R., & Stolz, S. B. (1982). Mental health promotion and the media. *American Psychologist, 37,* 1136–1139.

Glennon, L. M., & Butsch, R. (1982). The family as portrayed on television, 1946–1978. In D. Pearl, L. Bouthilet, & J. Lazar (Eds.), *Television and behavior: Ten years of scientific progress and implications for the eighties* (vol.2), *Technical reviews* (pp.264–271). Washington, DC: U. S. Government Printing Office.

Glick, I. O., & Levy, S. (1962). *Living with Television.* Chicago: Aldine.

Goldberg, M. E., & Gorn, G. J. (1974). Children's reactions to television advertising: An experimental approach. *Journal of Consumer Research, 1,* 69–75.

Goldberg, M. E., & Gorn, G. J. (1978). Some unintended consequences of TV advertising to children. *Journal of Consumer Research, 5,* 22–29.

Goldberg, M. E., Gorn, G., & Gibson, W. (1978). TV messages for snack and breakfast foods: Do they influence children's preferences? *Journal of Consumer Research, 5,* 73–81.

Gorn, G. J., & Florsheim, R. (1985). The effects of commercials for adult products on children. *Journal of Consumer Research, 11,* 962–967.

Gorn, G. J., & Goldberg, M. (1977). The impact of television advertising on children from low income families. *Journal of Consumer Research, 4,* 86–88.

Gorn, G. J., Goldberg, M. E., & Kanungo, R. N. (1976). The role of educational television in changing the intergroup attitudes of children. *Child Development, 47,* 277–280.

Gould, M. S., & Shaffer, D. (1986). The impact of suicide in television movies: Evidence of imitation. *New England Journal of Medicine, 315*(11), 690–694.

Graves, S. B. (1980). Psychological effects of black portrayals on television. In S. B. Withey & R. P. Abeles (Eds.), *Television and social behavior: Beyond violence toward children.* Hillsdale, NJ: Erlbaum.

Greenberg, B. S. (1972). Children's reactions to TV blacks. *Journalism Quarterly, 49*(1), 5–14.

Greenberg, B. S. (1974). Gratifications of television viewing and their correlates for British children. In J. G. Blumler & E. Katz (Eds.), *The uses of mass communications: Current perspectives on gratifications research* (pp.71–92). Beverly Hills, CA: Sage.

Greenberg, B. S. (1986). Minorities and the mass media. In J. Bryant & D. Zillmann (Eds.), *Perspectives on media effects* (pp.165–188). Hillsdale, NJ: Erlbaum.

Greenberg, B. S. (1988). Some uncommon television images and the drench hypothesis. In S. Oskamp (Ed.), *Applied social psychology annual* (vol. 8), *Television as a social issue* (pp.88–102). Beverly Hills, CA: Sage.

Greenberg, B. S., Buerkel-Rothfuss, N., Neuendorf, K., & Atkin, C. K. (1980). Three seasons of television family role interactions. In B. S. Greenberg (Ed.), *Life on television: Content analysis of U.S. TV Drama.* Norwood, NJ: Ablex.

Greenberg, B. S., & D'Alessio, D. (1985). Quantity and quality of sex in the soaps. *Journal of Broadcasting and Electronic Media, 29,* 309–321.

Greenberg, B. S., Linsangan, R. L., & Soderman, A. (1987). *Adolescents and their exposure to television and movie sex.* (Project CAST Rep. No. 4). East Lansing: Michigan State University, Department of Telecommunication.

Greenberg, B. S., Linsangan, R., Soderman, A., & Heeter, C. (1988). *Adolescents and their reactions to television sex.* (Project CAST Rep. No. 5). East Lansing: Michigan State University, Department of Telecommunication.

Greenfield, P. M. (1984). *Mind and media: The effects of television, video games, and computers.* Cambridge, MA: Harvard University Press.

Greer, D., Potts, R., Wright, J. C., & Huston, A. C. (1982). The effects of television commercial form and commercial placement on children's social behavior and attention. *Child Development, 53,* 611–619.

Gunter, B. (1981). Can television teach kindness? *Bulletin of the British Psychological Society, 34,* 121–124.

Gunter, B., & Svennevig, M. (1987). *Behind and in front of the screen: Television's involvement with family life.* London: John Libbey.

Guttentag, D.N.W., Albritton, W. L., & Kettner, R. B. (1983). Daytime television viewing by hospitalized children: The effect of alternate programming. *Pediatrics, 71*(4), 620–625.

Haffner, D. W., & Kelly, M. (1987). Adolescent sexuality in the media. In Center for Population Options (Ed.), *Transitions: Focus on youth and families.* Washington, DC: Author.

Harris and Associates (1987, February). *Attitudes about television, sex and contraceptive advertising.* New York: Harris and Associates.

Harrison, L. F., & Williams, T. M. (1986). Television and cognitive development. In T. M. Williams (Ed.), *The impact of television: A natural experiment in three communities* (pp.87–142). Orlando, FL: Academic Press.

Hawkins, R., & Pingree, S. (1982). Television's influence on social reality. In D. Pearl, L. Bouthilet, & J. Lazar (Eds.), *Television and behavior: Ten years of scientific progress and implications for the eighties* (vol.2), *Technical reviews* (pp.224–247). Rockville, MD: National Institute of Mental Health.

Himmelweit, H. T., Oppenheim, A. N., & Vince, P. (1958). *Television and the child: An empirical study of the effects of television on the young.* London: Oxford University Press.

Hollenbeck, A. R., & Slaby, R. G. (1979). Infant visual and vocal responses to television. *Child Development, 50,* 41–45.

Horton, H., & Stack, S. (1984). The effect of television on national suicide rates. *Journal of Social Psychology, 123,* 141–142.

Huesmann, L. R., & Eron, L. D. (Eds.). (1986). *Television and the aggressive child: A cross-national comparison.* Hillsdale, NJ: Erlbaum.

Huesmann, L. R., Eron, L. D., Lefkowitz, M. M., & Walder, L. O. (1984). Stability of aggression over time and generations. *Developmental Psychology, 20,* 1120–1134.

Huesmann, L. R., Eron, L. D., Klein, R., Brice, P., & Fischer, P. (1983). Mitigating the imitation of aggressive behaviors by changing children's attitudes about media violence. *Journal of Personality and Social Psychology, 44,* 899–910.

Huesmann, L. R., Lagerspetz, K., & Eron, L. D. (1984). Intervening variables in the television violence-viewing-aggression relation: Evidence from two countries. *Developmental Psychology, 20,* 746–775.

Huston, A. C., Greer, D., Wright, J. C., Welch, R., & Ross, R. (1984). Children's comprehension of televised formal features with masculine and feminine connotations. *Developmental Psychology, 20,* 707–716.

Huston, A. C., Watkins, B. A., & Kunkel, D. (1989). Public policy and children's television. *American Psychologist, 44,* 424–433.

Huston, A. C., & Wright, J. C. (1983). Children's processing of television: The informative functions of formal features. In J. Bryant & D. R. Anderson (Eds.), *Children's understanding of television: Research on attention and comprehension* (pp.35–68). New York: Academic Press.

Huston, A. C., & Wright, J. C. (1989). Television forms and children. In G. Comstock (Ed.), *Public Communication and Behavior* (vol.2) (pp.103–159). New York: Academic Press.

Huston, A. C., Wright, J. C., Rice, M. L., Kerkman, D., & St. Peters, M. (1990). The development of television viewing patterns in early childhood: A longitudinal investigation. *Developmental Psychology, 26,* 409–420.

Jerome, N. W. (1982). Advertising and food choice. *Proceedings: Lillian Fountain Smith Conference for Nutrition Educators* (pp.79–98). Fort Collins: Colorado State University.

Johnston, J., & Ettema, J. S. (1982). *Positive images: Breaking stereotypes with children's television.* Beverly Hills, CA: Sage.

Joy, L. A., Kimball, M., & Zabrack, M. L. (1986). Television exposure and children's aggressive behavior. In T. M. Williams (Ed.), *The impact of television: A natural experiment involving three towns* (pp.303–360). New York: Academic Press.

Katz, P. A. (1979). The development of female identity. In C. B. Kopp (Ed.), *Becoming female: Perspectives on development* (pp.3–28). New York: Plenum Press.

Katz, P. A., & Coulter, D. K. (1986). *Progress report: Modification of gender: Stereotyped behavior in children.* (Grant No. BNS-8316047). Washington, DC: National Science Foundation.

Kaufman, L. (1980). Prime time nutrition. *Journal of Communication, 30*(3), 37–46.

Keegan, C.A.V. (1983). Using television to reach older people with prevention messages: The over easy experiment. In J. Sprafkin, C. Swift, & R. Hess (Eds.), *Rx Television: Enhancing the preventive impact of TV* (pp.83–91). New York: Haworth Press.

Keilhacker, M. (Ed.). (1969). *Findings and cognition on the television perception of children and young people based on the prize-winning programmes of Prix Jeunesse 1966: Patrick and Putrick and Clown Ferdl.* Munich: Internationales Zentralinstitut fur das Jugend- und Bildungferensehen.

Kerkman, D., Kunkel, D., Huston, A. C., Wright, J. C., & Pinon, M. F. (1990). Children's Television Programming and the "Free Market Solution." *Journalism Quarterly, 67*(1), 147–156.

Kessler, R. C., & Stipp, H. (1984). The impact of fictional television suicide stories on U.S. fatalities: A replication. *American Journal of Sociology, 90,* 151–167.

Kimball, M. (1986). Television and sex-role attitudes. In T. M. Williams (Ed.), *The impact of television: A natural experiment in three communities* (pp. 265–301). Orlando, FL: Academic Press.

Kippax, S., & Murray, J. (1979). *Small screen, big business.* Sydney: Angus & Robertson.

Kippax, S., & Murray, J. P., (1980). Using the mass media: Need gratification and perceived utility. *Communication Research, 7,* 335–360.

Kovaric, P. (1987, April). *Children's alternatives to Nielsen categories of television programming and how they predict social reality beliefs.*

Paper presented at the biennial conference of the Society for Research in Child Development, Baltimore, MD.

Kovaric, P., Doubleday, C., & Dorr, A. (in preparation). Conceptualizing television messages about families' emotional health. In A. Dorr (Ed.), *Emotions and television*.

Krugman, H. D. (1971). Brainwave measures of media involvement. *Journal of Advertising Research, 11*, 3–9.

Kubey, R., & Csikszentmihalyi, M. (1990). *Television and the quality of life: How viewing shapes everyday experiences*. Hillsdale, NJ: Erlbaum.

Kubey, R. W. (1980). Television and aging: Past, present and future. *Gerontologist, 20*, 16–35.

Kunkel, D. (1988a). Children and host selling television commercials. *Communication Research, 15*, 71–92.

Kunkel, D. (1988b). From a raised eyebrow to a turned back: Regulatory factors influencing the growth of children's product-related programming. *Journal of Communication, 38*(4), 90–108.

Kunkel, D., & Watkins, B. (1987). Evolution of children's television regulatory policy. *Journal of Broadcasting and Electronic Media, 31*, 367–389.

Kunkel, D. L. (1987). *A survey of non-program content during children's programming on independent television stations*. Unpublished manuscript. University of California, Santa Barbara.

Laosa, L. M. (1976). Viewing bilingual multicultural educational television: An empirical analysis of children's behaviors during television viewing. *Journal of Educational Psychology, 68*, 133–142.

Leary, A., Wright, J. C., & Huston, A. C. (1985, April). *Young children's judgments of the fictional/nonfictional status of television programming*. Presented at the biennial meeting of the Society for Research in Child Development, Toronto, Canada.

Lefkowitz, M., Fron, L., Walder, L., & Huesmann, L. R. (1972). Television violence and child aggression: A follow up study. In G. A. Comstock & E. A. Rubinstein (Eds.), *Television and social behavior* (vol. 3), *Television and adolescent aggressiveness* (pp. 35–135). Washington, DC: U.S. Government Printing Office.

Lemish, D., & Rice, M. L. (1986). Television as a talking picture book: A prop for language acquisition. *Journal of Child Language, 13*, 251–274.

Lemnitzer, N. B., Jeffrey, D. B., Hess, M. J., Hickey, J. S., & Stroud, J. M. (1979, March). *Children's television food advertising: Does it affect eating behavior?* Paper presented at the meeting of the Society for Research in Child Development, San Francisco.

Lesser, G. S. (1974). *Children and television: Lessons from "Sesame Street."* New York: Random House.

Lesser, H. (1977). *Television and the preschool child.* New York: Academic Press.

Levi, L. (1965). The urinary output of adrenalin and nonadrenalin during pleasant and unpleasant emotional states: A preliminary report. *Psychosomatic Medicine, 27,* 80–85.

Levin, S., Petros, T., & Petrella, F. (1982). Preschoolers' awareness of television advertising. *Child Development, 53,* 933–937.

Liebert, D. E., Sprafkin, J. N., Liebert, R. M., & Rubinstein, E. A. (1977). Effects of television commercial disclaimers on the product expectations of children. *Journal of Communication, 27*(1), 118–124.

Liebert, R. M., & Baron, R. A. (1972). Short term effects of television aggression on children's aggressive behavior. In J. P. Murray, E. A. Rubinstein, & G. A. Comstock, (Eds.), *Television and social behavior* (vol.2), *Television and social learning* (pp.181–201). Washington DC: U.S. Government Printing Office.

Liebert, R. M., & Sprafkin, J. (1988). *The early window: Effects of television on children and youth* (3rd ed.). New York: Pergamon.

Linn, M. C., de Benedictis, T., & Delucchi, K. (1982). Adolescent reasoning about advertisements: Preliminary investigations. *Child Development, 53,* 1599–1613.

Linne, O. (1971, July). *Reactions of children to violence on TV.* Stockholm, Sweden: Sveriges Radio, Audience and Programme Research Department.

Linz, D., Donnerstein, E., & Penrod, S. (1987a). The findings and recommendations of the Attorney General's Commission on Pornography: Do the psychological facts fit the political fury? *American Psychologist, 42,* 946–953.

Linz, D., Donnerstein, E., & Penrod, S. (1987b). Sexual violence in the mass media: Social psychological implications. In P. Shaver & C. Hendrick (Eds.), *Review of Personality and Social Psychology* (vol.7). Beverly Hills, CA: Sage.

Lloyd-Kolkin, D., Wheeler, P., & Strand, T. (1980). Developing a curriculum for teenagers. *Journal of Communication, 30*(3), 119-125.

Loye, D., Gorney, R., & Steele, G. (1977). Effects of television: An experimental field study. *Journal of Communication, 27*(3), 206-216.

Lull, J. (1982). How families select television programs. A mass observational study. *Journal of Broadcasting, 26,* 801-811.

Macklin, M. C., & Kolbe, R. H. (1984). Sex role stereotyping in children's advertising: Current and past trends. *Journal of Advertising, 13*(2), 34-42.

Malamuth, N., & Donnerstein, E. (1982). The effects of aggressive-pornographic mass media stimuli. In L. Berkowitz (Ed.), *Advances in experimental social psychology* (vol.15, pp.104-136). New York: Academic Press.

Malamuth, N. M. (1986). Predictors of naturalistic sexual aggression. *Journal of Personality and Social Psychology, 50,* 953-962.

Malamuth, N. M., & Briere, J. (1986). Sexual violence in the media: Indirect effects of aggression against women. *Journal of Social Issues, 42,* 75-92.

Malamuth, N. M., & Check, J.V.P. (1980). Penile tumescence and perceptual responses to rape as a function of victim's perceived reactions. *Journal of Applied Social Psychology, 10,* 528-547.

Masters, J. C., Ford, M. E., & Arend, R. A. (1983). Children's strategies for controlling affective responses to aversive social experience. *Motivation and Emotion, 7,* 103-116.

McGee, P. E., & Frueh, T. (1980). Television viewing and the learning of sex-role stereotypes. *Sex Roles, 6,* 179-188.

McLeod, J. M., Fitzpatrick, M. A., Glynn, C. J., & Fallis, S. F. (1982). Television and social relations: Family influences and consequences for interpersonal behavior. In D. Pearl, L. Bouthilet, & J. Lazar (Eds.), *Television and behavior: Ten years of scientific progress and implications for the eighties* (vol.2), *Technical reviews* (pp.272-286). Washington, DC: U.S. Government Printing Office.

McLuhan, H. M. (1964). *Understanding media: The extensions of man.* New York: McGraw Hill.

Meadowcroft, J. M., & Zillmann, D. (1987). Women's comedy preferences during menstrual cycle. *Communications Research, 10,* 204-218.

Medoff, N. J. (1980, May). *The avoidance of comedy by persons in a negative affective state: A further study of selective exposure.* Paper presented at the annual conference of the International Communication Association, Acapulco.

Meehan, D. M. (1988). The strong-soft woman: Manifestations of the androgyne in popular media. *Applied Social Psychology Annual* (vol.8), *Television as a social issue* (pp.103–112). Newbury Park, CA: Sage.

Melamed, B. G., & Siegel, L. (1975). Reduction of anxiety in children facing hospitalization and surgery by use of filmed modeling. *Journal of Consulting and Clinical Psychology, 43,* 511–521.

Melody, W. (1973). *Children's TV: The economics of education.* New Haven: Yale University Press.

Messaris, P., & Hornik, R. C. (1983). Work status, television exposure, and educational outcomes. In C. Hayes & S. B. Kamerman (Eds.), *Children of working parents: Experiences and outcomes* (pp.44–72). Washington, DC: National Academy Press.

Meyer, T. P., Donohue, T. R., & Henke, L. L. (1978). How black children see TV commercials. *Journal of Advertising Research, 18*(5), 51–58.

Milavsky, J. R. (1980). Symposium on television entertainment: Response. *Character, 2*(1), 4–6.

Milavsky, J. R., Kessler, R. C., Stipp, H. H., & Rubens, W. S. (1982). *Television and aggression: A panel study.* New York: Academic Press.

Miller, W. (1985). A view from the inside: Brainwaves and television viewing. *Journalism Quarterly, 62,* 508–518.

Moore, R. L., & Stephens, L. F. (1975). Some communication and demographic determinants of adolescent consumer learning. *Journal of Consumer Research, 2,* 80–92.

Morgan, M. (1982). Television and adolescents' sex role sterotypes: A longitudinal study. *Journal of Personality and Social Psychology, 43,* 947–955.

Morgan, M. (1987). Television, sex-role attitudes, and sex-role behavior. *Journal of Early Adolescence, 7,* 269–282.

Morgan, M., Alexander, A., Shanahan, J., & Harris, C. (1990). Adolescents, VCRs, and the family environment. *Communication Research, 17,* 83–106.

Morgan, M., & Gross, L. (1982). Television and educational achievement and aspiration. In D. Pearl, L. Bouthilet, & J. Lazar (Eds.), *Television and behavior: Ten years of scientific progress and implications for the eighties* (vol.2), *Technical reports* (pp.78–90). Washington, DC: U.S. Government Printing Office.

Moss, M. (1987). The poverty story. *Columbia Journalism Review, 26,* 43–50.

Mulvey, E., & Haugaard, J. (1986). *Report of the Surgeon General's Workshop on Pornography and Public Health.* Washington, DC: U.S. Public Health Service.

Murray, J. P. (1973). Television and violence: Implications of the Surgeon General's research program. *American Psychologist, 28,* 472–478.

Murray, J. P. (1980). *Television and youth: 25 years of research and controversy.* Boys Town, NE: Boys Town Center for the Study of Youth Development.

Murray, J. P. (1984). Children and television violence. In J. P. Murray, & G. Salomon (Eds.), *The future of children's television: Results of the Markle Foundation/Boys Town Conference.* Boys Town, NE: Boys Town Center.

Murray, J. P. (1990). *Trends in the portrayal of families on U.S. commercial television, 1947-1987.* Unpublished manuscript, Kansas State University, Department of Human Development and Family Studies, Manhattan.

Murray, J. P., & Kippax, S. (1978). Children's social behavior in three towns with differing television experience. *Journal of Communication, 28*(1), 19–29.

Murray, J. P., & Kippax, S. (1981). From the early window to the late-night show: International trends in the study of the impact of television on children and adults. In L. Berkowitz, (Ed.), *Advances in experimental social psychology* (vol. 12). New York: Academic Press.

Murray, J. P., Rubinstein, E. A., & Comstock, G. A. (Eds.). (1972). *Television and social behavior* (vol.2), *Television and social learning.* Washington, DC: U.S. Government Printing Office.

Murray, J. P., & Salomon, G. (Eds.). (1984). *The future of children's television: Results of the Markle Foundation/Boys Town Conference.* Boys Town, NE: Boys Town Center.

Myersohn, R. (1961). A critical examination of commercial entertainment. In R. W. Kleemeier (Ed.), *Aging and Leisure.* New York: Oxford University Press.

National Commission on Working Women. (1982). *What's wrong with this picture? A look at working women on television.* Washington, DC: S. Steenland.

National Commission on Working Women. (1984). *The picture improves: A look at the 1984 television season.* Washington, DC: S. Steenland.

National Commission on Working Women. (1985). *Trouble on the set: An analysis of female characters on 1985 television programs.* Washington, DC: S. Steenland.

National Commission on Working Women. (1986a). *Prime time women: An analysis of older women on entertainment television.* Washington, DC: S. Steenland.

National Commission on Working Women. (1986b). *Women in focus: An analysis of TV's female characters and their jobs.* Washington, DC: S. Steenland.

National Institute of Mental Health. (1982). *Television and behavior: Ten years of scientific progress and implications for the eighties* (vol. 1), *Summary Report.* Washington DC: U.S. Government Printing Office.

Oskamp, S., King, J. C., Burn, S. M., Konrad, A. M., Pollard, J. A., & White, M. A. (1985). The media and nuclear war: Fallout from TV's The Day After. *Applied Social Psychology Annual, 6,* 127–158.

Paget, K. F., Kritt, D., & Bergemann, L. (1984). Understanding strategic interactions in television commercials: A developmental study. *Journal of Applied Developmental Psychology, 5,* 145–161.

Palmer, E. L. (1988). *Television and America's children: A crisis of neglect.* New York: Oxford University Press.

Palmer, E. L., Hockett, A. B., & Dean, W. W. (1983). The television family and children's fright reactions. *Journal of Family Issues, 4,* 279–292.

Palmer, E. L., & McDowell, C. N. (1979). Program/commercial separators in children's television programming. *Journal of Communication, 29*(3), 197–201.

Palmgreen, P., Wenner, L. A., & Rosengren, K. E. (1985). Uses and gratifications research: The past ten years. In K. E. Rosengren, L. A. Wenner, & P. Palmgreen (Eds.), *Media gratifications research: Current perspectives* (pp. 11–37). Beverly Hills, CA: Sage.

Palumbo, F. M., & Dietz, W. H., Jr. (1985). Children's television: Its effects on nutrition and cognitive development. *Pediatric Annals, 14,* 793–801.

Parke, R. D., Berkowitz, L., Leyens, J. P., West, S., & Sebastian, R. J. (1977). Some effects of violent and non-violent movies on the behavior of juvenile delinquents. In L. Berkowitz (Ed.), *Advances in Experimental Social Psychology* (vol. 10). New York: Academic Press.

Pearl, D., Bouthilet, L., & Lazar, J. (Eds.). (1982). *Television and behavior: Ten years of scientific progress and implications for the eighties* (vol.2), *Technical reviews.* Washington DC: U.S. Government Printing Office.

Peterson, J. L., Moore, K. A., & Furstenburg, F. F. (1984). *Television viewing and early initiation of sexual intercourse: Is there a link?* Paper presented at the annual meeting of the American Psychological Association, Toronto, Ontario, Canada.

Phillips, D. P. (1982). The impact of fictional television stories on U.S. adult fatalities: New evidence on the effect of the mass media on violence. *American Journal of Sociology, 87,* 1340–1359.

Phillips, D. P. (1983). The impact of mass media violence on U.S. homicides. *American Sociological Review, 48,* 560–568.

Phillips, D. P. (1986). Natural experiments on the effects of mass media violence on fatal aggression: Strengths and weaknesses of a new approach. In L. Berkowitz (Ed.). *Advances in Experimental Social Psychology* (vol.19). New York: Academic Press.

Phillips, D. P., & Carstensen, L. L. (1986). Clustering of teenage suicides after television news stories about suicide. *New England Journal of Medicine, 315,* 685–689.

Phillips, D. P., and Paight, B. A. (1987). The impact of televised movies about suicide: A replicative study. *New England Journal of Medicine, 317,* 809–811.

Phillips, S., Williams, T. M., & Travis, L. (1986, June). *Characteristics of children's TV in Canada and the use of TV by Canadian children.* Paper presented at the Annual Meeting of the Canadian Psychological Association, Toronto.

Pierce, C. M. (1980). Social trace contaminants: Subtle indicators of racism in TV. In S. B. Withey & R. P. Abeles (Eds.), *Television and social behavior: Beyond violence toward children.* Hillsdale, NJ: Erlbaum.

Pinon, M. F., Huston, A. C., & Wright, J. C. (1989). Family ecology and child characteristics that predict young children's educational television viewing. *Child Development, 60,* 846–856.

Poindexter, P. M., & Stroman, C. A. (1980). Blacks and television: A review of the research literature. *Journal of Broadcasting, 25,* 103–122.

Potts, R., Huston, A. C., & Wright, J. C. (1986). The effects of television form and violent content on boys' attention and social behavior. *Journal of Experimental Child Psychology, 41,* 1–17.

Resnick, A., & Stern, B. L. (1977). Children's television advertising and brand choice: A laboratory experiment. *Journal of Advertising, 6,* 11–17.

Rice, M. L., Huston, A. C., Truglio, R., & Wright, J. C. (1990). Words from Sesame Street: Learning vocabulary while viewing. *Developmental Psychology, 26,* 421–428.

Rice, M. L., & Sell, M. (1990). *Exploration of the uses and effectiveness of "Sesame Street" home videocassettes.* Unpublished manuscript, University of Kansas, Lawrence.

Ritchie, D., Price, V., & Roberts, D. F. (1987). Television, reading, and reading achievement: A reappraisal. *Communication Research, 14,* 292–315.

Roberts, D. F., & Bachen, C. M. (1981). Mass communication effects. *Annual Review of Psychology, 32,* 307–356.

Roberts, D. F., Christensen, P., Gibson, W. A., Mooser, L., & Goldberg, M. E. (1980). Developing discriminating consumers. *Journal of Communication, 30*(3), 94–105.

Roberts, E. J. (1982). Television and sexual learning in children. In D. Pearl, L. Bouthilet, & J. Lazar (Eds.), *Television and behavior: Ten years of scientific research and implications for the eighties* (vol.2), *Technical reports* (pp.209–223). Washington, DC: U.S. Government Printing Office.

Robertson, T. S., & Rossiter, J. R. (1974). Children and commercial persuasion: An attribution theory analysis. *Journal of Consumer Research, 1,* 13–20.

Robertson, T. S., & Rossiter, J. R. (1976). Short-run advertising effects on children: A field study. *Journal of Marketing Research, 13,* 68–80.

Robertson, T. S., & Rossiter, J. R. (1977). Children's responsiveness to commercials. *Journal of Communication, 27*(1), 101–106.

Robertson, T. S., Rossiter, J. R., & Gleason, T. C. (1979). Children's receptivity to proprietary medicine advertising. *Journal of Consumer Research, 6,* 247–255.

Roedder, D. H., Sternhal, B., & Calder, B. J. (1983). Attitude-behavior consistency in children's responses to television advertising. *Journal of Marketing Research, 20,* 337–349.

Rosengren, K. E., Wenner, L. A., & Palmgreen, P. (Eds.). (1985). *Media gratification research: Current perspectives.* Beverly Hills, CA: Sage.

Rosengren, K. E., & Windahl, S. (1989). *Media matter: TV use in childhood and adolescence.* Norwood, NJ: Ablex.

Ross, R. P., Campbell, T., Wright, J. C., Huston, A. C., Rice, M. L., & Turk, P. (1984). When celebrities talk, children listen: An experimental analysis of children's responses to TV ads with celebrity endorsement. *Journal of Applied Developmental Psychology, 5,* 185–202.

Rossiter, J. (1977). Reliability of a short test measuring children's attitudes toward television commercials. *Journal of Advertising Research, 3,* 179–184.

Rossiter, J., & Robertson, T. (1974). Children's television commercials: Testing the defenses. *Journal of Broadcasting, 23,* 33–40.

Rowland, W. D. (1983). *The politics of TV violence.* Beverly Hills, CA: Sage.

Rubinstein, E. A., Comstock, G. A., & Murray, J. P. (Eds.). (1972). *Television and social behavior* (vol.4), *Television in day-to-day life: Patterns of use.* Washington, DC: U.S. Government Printing Office.

Rubinstein, E. A., & Sprafkin, J. N. (1982). Television and persons in institutions. In D. Pearl, L. Bouthilet, & J. Lazar (Eds.), *Television and behavior: Ten years of scientific progress and implications for the eighties* (vol.2), *Technical reports* (pp.322–330). Washington, DC: U.S. Government Printing Office.

Rushton, J. P. (1979). Effects of prosocial television and film material on the behavior of viewers. In L. Berkowitz (Ed.), *Advances in Experimental Social Psychology* (vol.12, pp.322–351). New York: Academic Press.

Rushton, J. P. (1982). Television and prosocial behavior. In D. Pearl, L. Bouthilet, & J. Lazar (Eds.), *Television and behavior: Ten years of scientific progress and implications for the eighties* (vol.2), *Technical reports* (pp.248–258). Washington, DC: U.S. Government Printing Office.

Russo, V. (1981). *The celluloid closet: Homosexuality in the movies.* New York: Harper & Row.

Salomon, G. (1977). Effects of encouraging Israeli mothers to co-observe "Sesame Street" with their five-year-olds. *Child Development, 48,* 1146–1151.

Salomon, G. (1979). *Interaction of media, cognition, and learning.* San Francisco: Jossey-Bass.

Salomon, G. (1983). Television watching and mental effort: A social psychological view. In J. Bryant & D. R. Anderson (Eds.), *Children's understanding of television: Research on attention and comprehension* (pp.181-198). New York: Academic Press.

Schalinske, T. (1968). *The role of television in the life of the aged person.* Unpublished doctoral dissertation, Ohio State University, Columbus.

Schramm, W., Lyle, J., & Parker, E. B. (1961). *Television in the lives of our children.* Stanford: Stanford University Press.

Schuetz, S., & Sprafkin, J. (1979). Portrayal of prosocial and aggressive behaviors on children's TV commercials. *Journal of Broadcasting, 23,* 33-40.

Sheikh, A., & Moleski, L. (1977). Conflict in the family over commercials. *Journal of Communication, 27*(1), 152-157.

Siemicki, M., Atkin, D., Greenberg, B., & Baldwin, T. (1986). Nationally distributed children's shows: What cable TV contributes. *Journalism Quarterly, 63,* 710-718, 734.

Signorielli, N. (1987). Children and adolescents on television: A consistent pattern of devaluation. *Journal of Early Adolescence, 7,* 255-268.

Silverman, L. T., Sprafkin, J. N., & Rubinstein, E. A. (1979). Physical contact and sexual behavior in prime time TV. *Journal of Communication, 29,* 33-43.

Simpkins, J. D., & Brenner, D. J. (1984). Mass media communication and health. In B. Dervin & M. J. Voight (Eds.), *Progress in communication sciences* (vol.5, pp.275-297). Norwood, NJ: Ablex.

Singer, D. G., Singer, J. L., & Zuckerman, D. M. (1981a). *Getting the most out of TV,* Santa Monica, CA: Goodyear.

Singer, D. G., Singer, J. L., & Zuckerman, D. M. (1981b). *Teaching television: How to use TV to your child's advantage.* New York: Dial Press.

Singer, D. G., Zuckerman, D. M., & Singer, J. L. (1980). Helping elementary school children learn about TV. *Journal of Communication, 30*(3), 84-93.

Singer, J. L. (1980). The power and limits of television: A cognitive-affective analysis. In P. Tannenbaum (Ed.), *The entertainment function of television.* Hillsdale, NJ: Erlbaum.

Singer, J. L., & Singer, D. G. (1981). *Television, imagination and aggression: A study of preschoolers.* Hillsdale, NJ: Erlbaum.

Skill, T., Wallace, S., & Cassata, M. (1990). Families on prime-time television: Patterns of conflict escalation and resolution across intact, non-intact, and mixed-family settings. In J. Bryant (Ed.), *Television and the American family* (pp.129-164). Hillsdale, NJ: Erlbaum.

Solomon, D. S. (1982). Health campaigns on television. In D. Pearl, L. Bouthilet, & J. Lazar (Eds.), *Television and behavior: Ten years of scientific progress and implications for the eighties* (vol. 2), *Technical reviews* (pp.308-321). Washington, DC: U.S. Government Printing Office.

Sparks, G. G. (1986). Developmental differences in children's reports of fear induced by the mass media. *Child Study Journal, 16,* 55-66.

Sparks, G. G., & Cantor, J. (1986). Developmental differences in fright responses to a television program depicting a character transformation. *Journal of Broadcasting, 30,* 309-323.

Sprafkin, J. N., Gadow, K. D., & Grayson, P. (1984). Television and the emotionally disturbed, learning disabled, and mentally retarded child: A review. In K. P. Gadow (Ed.), *Advances in learning and behavioral disabilities* (vol.3, pp.151-213). Greenwich, CT: JAI Press.

Sprafkin, J. N., & Silverman, L. T. (1981). Update: Physically intimate and sexual behavior on primetime television: 1978-79. *Journal of Communication, 31,* 34-40.

St. Peters, M., Fitch, M., Huston, A. C., Wright, J. C., & Eakins, D. (1991). Television and families: What do young children watch with their parents? *Child Development, 62.*

St. Peters, M., Fitch, M., Wright, J. C., & Huston, A. C. (1989, April). *Parents and children viewing television together.* Paper presented at the biennial meeting of the Society for Research in Child Development, Kansas City, MO.

Staples, R., & Jones, T. (1985, May/June). Culture, ideology and black television images. *Black Scholar,* pp.10-20.

Stein, A. H., & Friedrich, L. K. (1972). Television content and young children's behavior. In J. P. Murray, E. A. Rubinstein, & G. A. Comstock (Eds.), *Television and social behavior* (vol. 2), *Television and social learning* (pp.202-317). Washington DC: U.S. Government Printing Office.

Stein, A. H., & Friedrich, L. K. (1975). Impact of television on children and youth. In E. M. Hetherington (Ed.), *Review of child development research* (vol.5, pp.183-256). Chicago: University of Chicago Press.

Stephens, N., & Stutts, M. A. (1982). Preschoolers' ability to distinguish between television programming and commercials. *Journal of Advertising, 11*(2), 16–26.

Stoneman, Z., & Brody, G. H. (1983). Immediate and long-term recognition and generalization of advertised products as a function of age and presentation mode. *Developmental Psychology, 19,* 56–61.

Sturm, H. (1975). The research activities of the Internationales Zentralinstitut fur das Jugend- und Bildungferensehen. *Fernsehen und Bildung, 9,* 158–162.

Sturm, H. (1978). Emotional effects—Media-specific factors in radio and television: Results of two studies and projected research. *Fernsehen und Bildung, 12,* 105–112.

Stutts, M. A., Vance, D., & Hudleson, S. (1981). Program-commercial separators in children's television: Do they help a child tell the difference between *Bugs Bunny* and the *Quik Rabbit*? *Journal of Advertising, 10,* 16–25.

Surgeon General's Scientific Advisory Committee on Television and Social Behavior. (1972). *Television and growing up: The impact of televised violence.* Washington, DC: U.S. Government Printing Office.

Taylor, E. (1987, October). TV families: Three generations of packaged dreams. *Boston Review, 12*(5), 5–6, 27–29.

Taylor, E. G., & Walsh, A. S. (1987). "And next week—child abuse!" Family issues in contemporary made-for-TV movies. In S. Thomas (Ed.), *Culture and Communication* (pp.168–177). Norwood, NJ: Ablex.

Thomas, M. H. (1982). Physiological arousal, exposure to a relatively lengthy aggressive film, and aggressive behavior. *Journal of Research in Personality, 16,* 72–81.

Thomas, M. H., Horton, R. W., Lippincott, E. C., & Drabman, R. S. (1977). Desensitization to portrayals of real-life aggression as a function of exposure to television violence. *Journal of Personality and Social Psychology, 35,* 450–458.

Thomas, S., & Callahan, B. P. (1982). Allocating happiness: TV families and social class. *Journal of Communication, 32,* 184–190.

Tower, R. B., Singer, D. G., Singer, J. L., & Biggs, A. (1979). Differential effects of television programming on preschoolers' cognition, imagination, and social play. *American Journal of Orthopsychiatry, 49,* 265–281.

Truglio, R. T. (1990, March). *What is television teaching adolescents about sexuality?* Paper presented at the meeting of the Society for Research on Adolescence, Atlanta, GA.

Truglio, R. T., Huston, A. C., & Wright, J. C. (1986, August). *The relation of children's print and television use to early reading skills: A longitudinal study.* Paper presented at the annual meeting of the American Psychological Association, Washington, DC.

Tucker, L. A. (1986). The relationship of television viewing to physical fitness and obesity. *Adolescence, 21,* 797–806.

Turow, J., & Coe, L. (1985). Curing television's ills: The portrayal of health care. *Journal of Communication, 35*(4), 36–51.

United States Commission on Civil Rights (1977). *Window dressing on the set: Women and minorities in television.* Washington DC: U.S. Government Printing Office.

Van Son, L. G. (Ed.). (1982). *Video in health.* White Plains, NY: Knowledge Industry Publications.

Vidmar, N., & Rokeach, M. (1974). Archie Bunker's bigotry: A study in selective perception and exposure. *Journal of Communication, 24*(1), 35–47.

Wakshlag, J. J., Vial V., & Tamborini, R. (1983). Selecting crime drama and apprehension about crime. *Human Communication Research, 10,* 227–242.

Wallack, L. M. (1983). Mass media campaigns in a hostile environment: Advertising as anti health education. *Journal of Alcohol and Drug Education, 28*(2), 51–63.

Ward, S. (1972). Childrens' reaction to commercials. *Journal of Advertising Research, 12*(2), 35–47.

Ward, S., Levinson, D., & Wackman, D. (1972). Children's attention to television advertising. In E. A. Rubinstein, G. A. Comstock, & J. P. Murray (Eds.), *Television and social behavior* (vol.4), *Television in day-to-day life: Patterns of use* (pp.491–515). Washington, DC: U.S. Government Printing Office.

Ward, S., Reale, G., & Levinson, D. (1972). Children's perceptions, explanations and judgments of television advertising: A further exploration. In E. A. Rubinstein, G. A. Comstock, & J. P. Murray (Eds.), *Television and social behavior* (vol.4), *Television in day-to-day life: Patterns of use* (pp.468–490). Washington, DC: U.S. Government Printing Office.

Ward, S., & Wackman, D. (1972). Children's purchase influence attempts and parental yielding. *Journal of Marketing Research, 9*, 316-319.

Ward, S., Wackman, D. B., & Wartella, E. (1977). *How children learn to buy: The development of consumer information processing skills.* Beverly Hills, CA: Sage.

Wartella, E., Heintz, K. E., Aidman, A. J., & Mazzarella, S. R. (1990). Television and beyond: Children's video media in one community. *Communication Research, 17*, 45-64.

Watkins, B., Calvert, S. L., Huston-Stein, A., & Wright, J. C. (1980). Children's recall of television material: Effects of presentation mode and adult labeling. *Developmental Psychology, 16*, 672-674.

Weigel, R. H., & Howes, P. W. (1982). Race relations on children's television. *The Journal of Psychology, 111*, 109-112.

Welch, R. L., Huston-Stein, A., Wright, J. C., & Plehal, R. (1979). Subtle sex-role cues in children's commercials. *Journal of Communication, 29*(3), 202-209.

Wells, W. D. (1965). Communicating with children. *Journal of Advertising Research, 5*(2), 2-14.

Wenner, L. (1976). Functional analysis of TV viewing for older adults. *Journal of Broadcasting, 20*, 77-88.

Wenner, L. A. (1985). The nature of news gratifications. In K. E. Rosengren, L. A. Wenner, & P. Palmgreen (Eds.), *Media gratifications research: Current perspectives* (pp.171-194). Beverly Hills, CA: Sage.

Williams, M., & Condry, J. (1989). *Living color: Minority portrayals and cross-racial interactions on television.* Paper presented at the meeting of the Society for Research in Child Development, Kansas City, MO.

Williams, P. A., Haertel, E. H., Walberg, H. J., & Haertel, G. D. (1982). The impact of leisure-time television on school learning: A research synthesis. *American Educational Research Journal, 19*, 19-50.

Williams, T. M. (Ed.). (1986). *The impact of television: A natural experiment in three communities.* New York: Academic Press.

Williams, T. M., Baron, D., Phillips, S., Travis, L., & Jackson, D. (1986, August). *The portrayal of sex roles on Canadian and U.S. television.* Paper presented to the working group on sex roles at the conference of the International Association for Mass Communication Research, New Delhi, India.

Wilson, B. J., & Cantor, J. (1985). Developmental differences in empathy with a television protagonist's fear. *Journal of Experimental Child Psychology, 39,* 284-299.

Winick, C., Williamson, L., Chuzmir, S., & Winick, M. (1973). *Children's television commercials: A content analysis.* New York: Praeger.

Winn, M. (1987). *Unplugging the plug-in drug.* New York: Penguin.

Wober, J. M. (1987). *Evaluating the broadcast campaign on AIDS.* London: Independent Broadcasting Authority.

Wright, J. C., & Huston, A. C. (1983). A matter of form: Potentials of television for young viewers. *American Psychologist, 38,* 835-843.

Wright, J. C., Kunkel, D., Pinon, M., & Huston, A. C. (1989). Children's affective and cognitive reactions to televised coverage of the space shuttle disaster. *Journal of Communication, 39*(2), 27-45.

Wright, J. C., St. Peters, M., & Huston, A. C. (1990). Family television use and its relation to children's cognitive skills and social behavior. In J. Bryant (Ed.), *Television and the American family* (pp.227-252). Hillsdale, NJ: Erlbaum.

Wroblewski, R., & Huston, A. C. (1987). Televised occupational stereotypes and their effects on early adolescents: Are they changing? *Journal of Early Adolescence, 7,* 283-297.

Zillmann, D. (1982). Television and arousal. In D. Pearl, L. Bouthilet, & J. Lazar (Eds.), *Television and behavior: Ten years of scientific progress and implications for the eighties* (vol.2), *Technical reports* (pp.53-67). Washington, DC: U.S. Government Printing Office.

Zillmann, D. (1985). The experimental exploration of gratifications from media entertainment. In K. E. Rosengren, L. A. Wenner, & P. Palmgreen (Eds.), *Media gratifications research: Current perspectives* (pp.225-240). Beverly Hills, CA: Sage.

Zillmann, D., & Bryant, J. (1984). Effects of massive exposure to pornography. In N. Malamuth & E. Donnerstein (Eds.), *Pornography and Sexual Aggression* (pp.115-138). New York: Academic Press.

Zillmann, D., Hezel, R. T., & Medoff, N. J. (1980). The effect of affective states on selective exposure to televised entertainment fare. *Journal of Applied Social Psychology, 10,* 322-339.

Zillmann, D., Mody, B., & Cantor, J. (1974). Empathetic perception of emotional displays in films as a function of hedonic and excitatory state prior to exposure. *Journal of Research in Personality, 8,* 335-349.

Zillmann, D., Weaver, J. B., Mundorf, N., & Aust, C. (1986). Effects of an opposite-gender companion's affect to horror on distress, delight, and attraction. *Journal of Personality and Social Psychology, 51,* 586–594.

Zuckerman, D. M., Singer, D. G., & Singer, J. L. (1980). Children's television viewing, racial and sex-role attitudes. *Journal of Applied Social Psychology, 10*(4), 281–294.

About the Authors

Aletha C. Huston is professor of human development and psychology and co-director of the Center for Research on the Influences of Television on Children (CRITC) at the University of Kansas, Lawrence.

Ed Donnerstein is professor and chair, Department of Communication, University of California at Santa Barbara.

Halford H. Fairchild, Ph.D. is past national president of the Association for Black Psychologists.

Norma D. Feshbach is professor and co-director of the NIMH Program in Applied Human Development, Department of Education and Psychology, University of California at Los Angeles.

Phyllis Katz is director of the Institute for Research on Social Problems, Boulder, Colorado.

John P. Murray is professor and department head, Human Development and Family Studies, Kansas State University, Manhattan.

Eli A. Rubinstein is adjunct research professor in mass communications, University of North Carolina, Chapel Hill.

Brian L. Wilcox is director, Office of Legislative Affairs and Policy Studies, American Psychological Association.

Diana Zuckerman is a professional staff member in the United States Congress.

Subject Index

This book was typeset in
Linotype Sabon by Impressions,
printed by Thomson-Shore, Inc.,
and designed by Dika Eckersley